MW00324053

LESSONS FROM LUTE

LESSONS FROM LUTE

Reflections on Legendary
Arizona Basketball
Coach Lute Olson

Steve Rivera

TRIUMPH
BOOKS

Library of Congress Cataloging-in-Publication Data

Names: Rivera, Steve, author.
Title: Lessons from Lute: reflections on legendary Arizona basketball coach Lute Olson / Steve Rivera.
Description: Chicago: Triumph Books, [2022]
Identifiers: LCCN 2022021772 | ISBN 9781629379982 (hardcover)
Subjects: LCSH: Olson, Lute. | Basketball coaches—United States—Biography. | Arizona Wildcats (Basketball team)—History. | University of Arizona—Basketball—History. | College sports—Arizona—History. | BISAC: SPORTS & RECREATION / Coaching / Basketball | BIOGRAPHY & AUTOBIOGRAPHY / Sports
Classification: LCC GV884.O45 R58 2022 | DDC 304.800934—dc23/eng/20220519
LC record available at https://lccn.loc.gov/2022021772

This book is available in quantity at special discounts for your group or organization. For further information, contact:

Triumph Books LLC
814 North Franklin Street
Chicago, Illinois 60610
(312) 337-0747
www.triumphbooks.com

Printed in U.S.A.
ISBN: 978-1-62937-998-2
Design by Patricia Frey

To my great sons, Cameron and Trey, who make me very proud to be their dad. And to my mom, Josie, who continues to be a huge supporter in so many ways.

Contents

Foreword

Through the years I've had the pleasure of being around some great basketball minds because of my father's background and then during my college and professional basketball days. I'm thankful for getting to be around them and learning from all of them. Thankfully, too, I've played for some very good coaches and a couple of Hall of Famers in Phil Jackson and, of course, Lute Olson.

I can't say enough about Coach O's influence on me and what he meant to me in those years at Arizona. He was tough, demanding, and caring—just what you ask for in a coach, a mentor. I'm sure my former teammates and those before me and after me would say the same. He was an imposing and striking man, but we all know that. When he spoke to you, you knew you needed to listen.

We all learned lessons from him. Probably each player had different ones or the same ones in different forms. I'm glad I was part of his life, and he was part of mine. In fact, I spent five years at Arizona and still consider them some of the best times of my life. While in school I once joked I wished I could spend five more there. Those were great, fun years playing for Coach O. And there was a lot of winning!

Heck, every time I go back to Tucson, I still think I'm gonna see him. It blows my mind. I miss him, we all miss him. But we are all very grateful and blessed that we got to learn from him and that we had the life experience that we had in Tucson. In fact, I thought the celebration of life event they had in McKale Center was awesome. That was proof he had an incredible impact on so many lives. I am grateful to have been part of a little window of his time because he helped shape me into the man I am today.

This book Steve Rivera has written tells the stories of those impacted by Coach O. Enjoy their stories. Here is mine: when Coach started coming to my high school games, I was blown away by it. But there were no real interactions at that time. There, however, was definitely a presence about him. He was easy to be around, but it was like in a grandfather-type way. You don't mess around with Grandpa Walton and you have an enormous level of respect for him.

I first got close to Coach Olson when the Hall of Famer visited the San Diego area to have an in-home visit with my family. He first came to my father's house and then my mother's house. We had a great time and a great talk. He and my dad were telling old stories as well, and then we got in our cars and we drove to my mom's house, where my mom had a bottle of wine ready. They had it together while we talked about Arizona. You could tell family was very important to him. When we were at my mom's, he was telling stories about his kids and Bobbi and everything else. He talked about how he ran the program, how he ran the team. When you're looking to move away from home for the first time, it's important that you get to somebody that actually cares. It was very clear that Coach cared about the kids who came to play for him. You could tell that he enjoyed a good, casual conversation, but that he was also very serious about what he did. He was very comforting to be around. And at the time, I was 17 or 18 years old.

Because of my dad, I was used to being in the company of high-profile basketball figures. Coach O had that same presence. You also knew you had better be on your best behavior when you were around him. It wasn't like a threatening way. It was more because of who he was as a person.

When I made my first visit to Arizona, Ricky Anderson and Richard Jefferson were also on the trip. I had absolutely loved watching those Miles Simon, Jason Terry, Mike Bibby, and Mike Dickerson teams play. I fell in love with Arizona basketball with how they were playing. So, Arizona was my clear No. 1 choice, but I had never been to Tucson. Bibby and Simon took me around. They were playing pickup basketball one Friday night, and my experience in Tucson was everything I hoped it would be. At that moment, there was no reason to even go look at any other school because Arizona was everything for me. During the visit Jefferson told me I should just commit right now, and I said, "I'm in 100 percent."

When Coach O took me to the airport in the morning, we sat at a corner restaurant, and he said he would love a commitment right then and that he had only two scholarship spots available. I shook his hand and said, "Consider me one of them." He said he couldn't wait to have me there and wished me safe travels back. By the time I had landed in San Diego, Jefferson had committed, too.

Even though I was the son of Bill Walton, I wasn't given special treatment. When you get there and you're a freshman, life is hard. You go through the recruiting process, and then the reality of it is you question what you are doing. You're 18 and you don't know any better. I broke my foot that first year, so I ended up redshirting. It was hard. But then you also see what he did, and everything had a purpose. Every one of us, who stuck it out, got better. And we grew our bond together. It was tighter and closer. He was the Godfather of it all.

He knew exactly what he was doing. He was challenging us. There were no excuses. It didn't matter who my father was. It didn't matter that Jefferson was a McDonald's All-American or that Anderson's dad played for him. The only thing that mattered was that we were on time for practice and events and that we did the work and played how he wanted us to play.

If we messed up, we were punished. The team would have to run miles at 5:00 AM. If you were in the starting lineup, you'd have to sit out half the game or you'd have to come off the bench. He stuck to it. That's how it was day after day. The younger you were, the tougher it was, but as you got older, he'd give you more leeway. He gave you more freedom. As the team became our own, I don't think we would have been ready for it had he not been hard on us.

In 2000 and then 2001, Arizona was one of the best teams in the country. In 2000 Arizona was the No. 1 overall seed in the NCAA Tournament, eventually losing to Wisconsin in the second round. With everyone back Arizona started the 2000–01 season ranked No. 1. It was only the second time in school history that had happened. The 1997–98 team marked the first time. Expectations were high with me, Jefferson, Gilbert Arenas, Jason Gardner, Loren Woods, and Michael Wright as the key contributors. He had his hands full with the talent we had. He had to deal with the egos of the stars of the team and their talents and he still had holdovers from teams from the past in Eugene Edgerson and Justin Wessel, who were both on the 1997 national title team.

Then there was the passing of Lute's longtime wife, Bobbi. That was the most challenging of it all. Bobbi was the mother of the team. And she was everything to Coach O. She was amazing to us since we were just young men living away from home for the first time. She had that motherly sense. She was always available to talk. And she'd say if Coach was in a bad mood not to worry about it because she'd take care of him. Sure enough, she did. And then we lost her in the middle of the season and then we lost Coach for a while because he left to grieve and be with family. If we hadn't had the foundation Coach O had already put into place, it could have made a talented team waste a year or miss on an opportunity to win a title. Instead it helped the team get closer, bond, and go on this great run toward a championship.

Before the great run, Olson came back after some thought he wouldn't return at all. It was tough for him, but it was my feeling that he needed basketball as a distraction. And obviously we needed him. I do think he had pain because his wife had just passed. You could feel it and see it in him. He was usually joyous and great to be around. You could see when he came back that it wasn't that same carefree environment we had as players. Coach was always serious about things, but we as players were aware of his situation and—because of our love for him and Bobbi—we all felt his pain. It got to a point where we wanted to win for Bobbi and for Lute.

Arizona ended up losing to Duke in the national championship game. A year later, the Wildcats were good again but didn't start the season in the top 25, breaking Arizona's streak of being in the polls for 14 consecutive seasons. We used that as motivation, and a couple of weeks into the season, Arizona was back in the top 10, going from unranked to No. 8 after winning the Coaches vs. Cancer Classic and beating Maryland and Florida. Other people were calling it a rebuild, but we had Gardner, Channing Frye, Salim Stoudamire, and success never really stopped.

And it revved up the next year when Arizona started No. 1 to begin the season for just the third time in school history. We were no worse than No. 4 all year in a season where Arizona was No. 1 for 13 weeks. That's the longest any UA team had been No. 1. We all came back and added Hassan Adams and Andre Iguodala. Anderson and Gardner had been with us a long time. We had all the experience we needed to be special. We had one goal, and that was to win the title. It didn't happen, but I saw the near return of the coach I remembered after the passing of Bobbi. I don't think you fully recover from something like that, but I'd say he was somewhere in between what he was and the new Lute. He was definitely more of himself than he was in 2001. How do you fully come back from losing someone who meant so much to you?

Through my years with Coach O, I learned responsibility, work ethic, the importance of the details of the game, and the importance of repetition. Those are life lessons that can be used forever.

Gardner and Arenas were late to practice once and they didn't start one game. Coach had his consequences. It didn't matter who you were. It was about doing things right and a certain way. It wasn't like you'd get cut out of the family, but you'd get punished. You had to do it the way he had set it up. And as a young person, that's how you learn. It's easy to live life when you're with your parents, but when you're with a bunch of other 18 year olds with a bunch of distractions, it's easy to get in trouble and act up. We continued to learn that lesson as we grew.

I appreciated those times. I also appreciated the times Lute Olson would find time to go see me play while I was playing for the Los Angeles Lakers. When our parents would go see us play, they had this joy when we were out there. Coach O obviously didn't have that when he was coaching us, but when he'd go see us play after we left—like when I'd play Jefferson when he was with the New Jersey Nets—you'd see the same joy on his face that we saw in our parents when we were playing for him.

In Coach's final months, I found time to visit and spend some time with him. We'd watch golf, we'd tell old stories, and we'd laugh. It was awesome. I wish I could have stayed there all day long.

—*Luke Walton*
Arizona forward, 1999–2002
NBA player, 2003–13
NBA head coach, 2016–21

Introduction

When someone suggested I write a book on Lute Olson, I wondered why I hadn't thought of it already. Maybe his passing had been too soon—August of 2020—and I needed some time to reflect on it. But what an idea to honor a man who had an impact on my life and so many others' lives. I say my life because I covered the regal and towering man for 17 of his 25 seasons while I was with the *Tucson Citizen*. And another few years when I was with FOX Sports Arizona.

Few would know of me had I not covered such a successful program. Not once did I cover a losing season. What I realized in covering his program was that coaching mattered. Leadership mattered. It's as important as good talent and good people. And that was the core of Olson's program. Good people plus good talent with strong leadership makes for winning teams and experiences.

I spent a lot of time with the Hall of Fame coach, traveling to games all over the country. And then I spent plenty of private time in the final decade of his life, doing lunches, book signings, and watching games. I'll forever cherish those times. At the end of the day, I was with a guy who loved basketball—coaching and watching—and loved his players.

But what would be the format for a book on him? Who would be available to speak about a coach, a father figure, a mentor, a friend, and so much more? It wasn't so easy to chase players and a coach or two down, but the likes of former Kansas and North Carolina coach Roy Williams stepped in as did longtime Stanford coach Mike Montgomery, who brought a great fight to Arizona's dominance in the conference for a number of years.

Coach O—as many players called him—put Tucson, the once dusty town, on the map for good when he brought his style of basketball to the Sonoran Desert. It was about being tough, disciplined, aggressive, fun, and, of course, successful. Guys like Steve Kerr, Sean Elliott, Miles Simon, Richard Jefferson, and Tom Tolbert arrived at Arizona as young freshmen and left as men and pretty darn good basketball players, many of whom became very good NBA players. "Everybody here was impacted by him so dramatically," Kerr said. "My life changed in an incredible fashion after coming to UA and playing for Coach O, learning everything I did from him. My whole professional career in basketball is really thanks to Coach."

From the early days of the toughest practices to the later years of success in the NCAA Tournaments, Olson was the guide of the Arizona ship that played in the tournament in 23 of the 25 years he was at Arizona. He was absent in his final official year. The NCAA Tournament was his home in March, and 1997 was his "One Shining Moment" as Arizona became the first—and still only—team to beat three No. 1 seeds to win the title. They did it with Simon, Mike Bibby, Jason Terry, Michael Dickerson, A.J. Bramlett, and Bennett Davison running and jumping their way to an improbable finish.

It was one of 589 wins Olson had at Arizona, and all were important and impactful. Players and coaches will attest to his competitiveness and demand of excellence. They'll say how he impacted them, how he motivated them, and how he loved them. "I can say I am who I am because of him," said Pete Williams, one of Arizona's first key recruits. "He is my rock, my go-to when things are tough, and my vow has always been and will continue to be to make him proud. I do that by living my life the right way and treating people the way I expect to be treated. I love him like you couldn't believe!"

They all learned from their beloved coach, the white-haired Hall of Famer who shaped and molded many of their successful futures. "I love Coach O," Bibby said, "great coach, even better human being."

In these pages Bibby and many other coaches and players will share in great depth what Coach Olson meant to them and the lessons he imparted.

1
Sean
Elliott

He's the Arizona basketball GOAT. Sean Elliott was Lute Olson's best player and is the school's all-time leading scorer. And it's not even close. The timing couldn't have been any better for Elliott's arrival—or Olson's. The latter arrived on campus in the spring of 1983. Elliott showed up on campus in 1985–86. Elliott was a hometown kid with big-time dreams. It was a match made in college basketball heaven and one that sent the Olson-led program into the clouds. "Lute was everything to me," Elliott said. "He gave me my foundation as a player. I had great high school coaches, but Coach, after four years under him, took me to the next level. And he just didn't do it for me but for all of us. What everyone will tell you is he gave us a foundation that carried us not just through our basketball careers but well after. We all have Coach Olson's way of thinking, the way he looked at the game, the fundamentals. All that was ingrained in us. Of course, the sense of team as well. That was so important. It's a permanent fixture in me. That's the best thing anyone could have ever done for me because he gave me a great foundation. Other coaches I had built on that."

When Olson arrived in that spring of 1983, Elliott had no inkling of being a Wildcat—even if the campus was just miles away from his house. Elliott was 15 at the time—and, yes, a basketball junkie, as he put it—and he knew of the great UA teams of the past, ones that featured Bob Elliott (no relation), Herman Harris, etc. But those teams were in the 1970s. "My early years before high school, Arizona was very good," Elliott said.

Then Fred Snowden was replaced with Ben Lindsey for one year before Olson was hired. "I always tell this story where I went to an Oregon game," Elliott said. "It was the season Arizona was 4–24. I had nosebleed seats, and by the end of the game, the ushers had taken me down to the second row because there was no one there, literally 200 to 300 people at the game."

It all changed when Robert Luther Olson—the man most everyone called Lute or Coach—arrived in Tucson and eventually declared McKale Center would be the place to be during the men's basketball season. "I managed to get tickets about the time it became the hottest ticket in town," Elliott said. "He had told people, 'Get your tickets now!' That's when I thought, maybe, just maybe, I'd go to UA. It was a possibility."

Elliott also admitted he hadn't been heavily recruited given that UTEP and Arizona State were the lone schools that had contacted him in his early high school years. "I had big dreams to go play somewhere else," Elliott said. "But by the time it was time to turn the program around, it didn't make sense for me to go somewhere else."

By then, Elliott was a year removed from meeting Olson at his annual summer camp. Elliott could sense a program being established. "Everyone who lived through that time felt the excitement," Elliott said. "You'd see Coach on TV and you'd see how he carried himself. He already came from Iowa. He'd taken them

Sean Elliott
(AP Images)

to the Final Four, so he had some gravitas, the way he turned it around so quickly, and you could see the excitement. I started to think, *Well, maybe this is the place if I'm ever going to be good enough to play here.*"

Little did anyone know that former player Pete Williams would have an impact on Elliott's recruitment. Back in 1985 when Arizona had a possible chance to win its first Pac-10 title, Williams and a few others got in trouble by breaking curfew on a trip to Washington. Olson suspended a couple of the players, eventually costing the team the chance at that title. Later that season, Olson arrived at his office to see a letter on his desk from Sean's mother, Odiemae Elliott, to say Olson was the ideal coach to play for given his integrity.

To get the attention of college coaches, though, Elliott would have to perform well on the summer camp circuit. "My sophomore, then junior year, I went to the Five-Star Basketball Camp, and it was the only way you could get noticed at the time," Elliott said. "When I got back my junior year, I started getting letters but mostly from kind of small schools. I was getting a lot of letters from [mid-major schools]."

After his junior year, he went back to Five-Star again. This time he went for two weeks and made the All-Star team. "Then I got a bunch of letters and got calls all the time," he said. "But by then I had pretty much made up my mind that I was going to Arizona."

Elliott did consider UTEP, but Arizona was always really the school for him. "It was meant to be," he said. "To be honest, I really liked UTEP because they were the first ones to call me right before anybody else. Coach Don Haskins did a great job

24

with that program. So, I was thinking UTEP, thinking I could get the offer and go there and play. But I'm so thankful I made the right decision because it just wasn't about basketball but the friendships and the people that I met along the way. I highly doubt I'd have those kinds of relationships and same kind of Arizona family feel if I had gone somewhere else. It's my hometown. My mom, father, brother got to go to the games. It was a great experience for all of them, too."

This thinnish kid, who could play, arrived on campus. And no sooner had he arrived that Olson put a lot on his shoulders. Elliott embraced that pressure. "It was great. I loved it," he said. "I really made strides, huge strides from the very first day of practice to the end of the year. So, it felt good. I was already a confident player by then. After high school I was really confident and felt like I could play anywhere and play with anybody. So, I just had to figure it out that first year as a freshman, and once I was able to do that, it felt good that Coach trusted me like he did."

Of course, there were challenges as well. They came his sophomore year when Arizona struggled a bit. A big reason was that the team's leader, Steve Kerr, was out with a knee injury. Much of the leadership was put on others, including Elliott. The first game didn't start off well. Arizona lost to UNLV 92–87 in Las Vegas. The game went down to the final moments, and Olson designed a play for someone, but Elliott decided to try to take the game over. It didn't go well.

After the game Olson lit into Elliott. "I broke the play and shot the ball," Elliott said. "I had just come from playing on Team USA with Coach Olson as the coach. He yelled at me, saying, 'You don't trust your teammates? You think you can do it by yourself?' That was the first time somebody had ever gone at me like that. I felt terrible. I mean, I was in tears."

It, though, served as a learning lesson. "I couldn't go at it alone," he said. "I had to do what Coach asked me to do. And there was a reason why he was running the play. He wanted it to run his way. And at the time, I had to realize I wasn't good enough to take over a game and break off a play and try to do it myself."

That was the opening game of his sophomore year, a difficult year for Elliott, Olson, and the program. "I've talked about this with my family and some friends a bit through the years," Elliott said. "But I wanted to transfer that year. To say Coach was on my ass is sugarcoating it…There were times that year—maybe three or four times—I'd go home and cry. One day coach Scott Thompson called me, and I told him that it felt that Coach didn't like me because he was on my ass all the time. Coach Thompson said to me, 'Does he yell at this guy?' I said no. 'Does he yell at that guy?' I said no…'He yells at you because he cares. He does it because he wants you to be great.' He said, 'You'd better start to worry when he quits yelling at you.' That was a lesson that I repeat to my kids and tell people. He was criticizing me because he loved me. You criticize when you want them to be better. You're correcting them. You want them to do better. I took that to heart."

Before that conversation he called his mom to say he was going to transfer. "She said, 'Boy, you're not going anywhere.' She all but said, 'Your ass isn't going anywhere. You're staying here.' I had to tough it out," Elliott said. "It would have been a stupid decision to go anywhere, an immature thing to do from a kid who didn't know better or didn't see the benefits of it."

Arizona finished 18–12 overall and made it into the NCAA Tournament but lost in the first round. Ironically, it was to UTEP. "I felt like there were times where I really played well that year," he said. "I started to blossom a little bit more as a player."

Elliott was given more freedom his junior year, and in that magical year of 1987–88, seemingly nothing could go wrong for Arizona. Kerr was back, and he and Elliott were surrounded by Tom Tolbert, Anthony Cook, Craig McMillan, Kenny Lofton, among others. Still, there were no discussions—private or otherwise—between Elliott and Olson about Elliott's role.

"He wasn't like that; he was Coach O," Elliott said. "Coach wasn't trying to be your friend at the time. That wasn't how he operated. One day in practice, he drew up a play for me in a late-game situation…it was an isolation play. That was kind of my play. Whenever the game was tight, he'd call that play. That would give me a lot of confidence. I'd catch the ball in front of our bench, and he'd say, 'Take 'em, take 'em!' When a coach has that kind of confidence in you, you think you're all-world."

Then the fun started. Arizona won 12 consecutive games, winning the Great Alaska Shootout by beating tough Michigan and Syracuse teams in back-to-back games. People started to see UA had something special. By the end of 1987, Arizona raced up the rankings to No. 1 in the country after beating Duke. "He was having a good time," Elliott said. "It all came out of nowhere. Remember: we started the season unranked. We beat Iowa at Iowa, and that was huge. I'm sure he was having a ball."

Olson often talked about there being an East Coast bias. Elliott believes there is one. "What he wanted was for our guys to get the recognition we deserved," Elliott said. "He also wanted our recruits to look our way and have Arizona as an option."

Eventually, Arizona went 17–1 in the Pac-10 and went to its first Final Four in 1988.

After the season Elliott was contemplating jumping to the NBA. While on a trip to Los Angeles as a finalist for the John R. Wooden Award, Elliott and Olson took in a game to watch the Lakers play the Seattle SuperSonics. "I'll never forget it," Elliott said. "We were about 30 rows up before a couple of ushers saw us and recognized us. They moved us down to some open seats that were in the third or fourth row behind the basket."

What Elliott saw was a bunch of men "massacring each other. I was in shock," Elliott said. "The physical play was astounding. I remember thinking, *I'm not ready for that. I'm not even close.* This wasn't like playing Washington State."

It was then he figured he had to come back for his final year. Hell, he joked, he probably needed another year after that because he was still a young student for his class. He then had a conversation with then-assistant-coach Kevin O'Neill, who asked him if he had been in a pickup game with pros. That was serious business. O'Neill said, "Those guys try to kill you."

By then, he realized he needed one more year. And by then, Arizona had celebrated its Final Four appearance and returned to a parade and a celebration at Arizona Stadium in front of thousands of fans. Olson even danced in the only way Olson could dance. "We kind of laughed because he let his hair down just a little bit," Elliott said. "But when you got away from the fans and the public when you're done playing and you come back [later in life], you really got to see Coach have a good time."

Elliott said he recalled going to New York to pick up a national award and Lute Olson, Bobbi Olson, Elliott's then-girlfriend, and Odiemae were in a smallish limousine. Olson sat in the front. "All of a sudden, the partition came down, and there was Coach O with a few mini whiskeys. He's passing them back, and we're all drinking. I was thinking, *I'm having alcohol with Coach Olson!* That was he craziest thing to me. I couldn't believe it. It was awesome."

Before that limo ride, Elliott still had to play his senior year. Of course, Elliott was a unanimous All-American leading the nation's No. 1 team. But Arizona fell in the Sweet 16 to UNLV on a last-second shot. "More than anything," Elliott said, "you want to win that Vegas game because there was some animosity between him and Tark at the time. We had beaten them at our place earlier in the year. So, we all wanted to win that game again. Unfortunately, it didn't work out for us. It's still painful to me, to be honest. We thought we had the best team. And had we won that game with everybody that was left in the tournament, I don't think that there was any doubt that we win it all. Even more so than the year before."

Elliott was drafted third overall in the 1989 NBA Draft by the San Antonio Spurs. "I'd come back to Coach's basketball camp and do the demonstrations. And we'd talk about my time in San Antonio and playing for Larry Brown and what Larry Brown wanted me to do and what I wanted to do," he said, laughing. "But Coach was always encouraging. He told me to keep working. And he would remind me that I was a really good player. And that's what I needed because…my rookie year Larry just tore me down. There was a whole different attitude when I got there. I wasn't really allowed to shoot it. I would get chewed out, and that was tough for me. My confidence was taken away from me. When I'd see Coach in the summertime or talk to him on the phone, he would remind me that I was a creator, that I could beat people. He'd remind me of all that."

Elliott, who became an NBA All-Star and champion, would return to U of A for visits. "It was fantastic," he said. "It was always so good, going to Coach's house, hanging out with him. Coach loved his wine. And so do I. So it was always great to get together with him and talk a little bit of wine and some basketball. It was great because I thought of him as a deity, like a god to us. To be around him and find out he's cool—I remember being with Anthony Cook one time, and we were all together. We left the house, and Anthony said, 'Coach Olson is *cool!*' I said, 'Yeah, he's just a cool dude.'…You kind of wish you had known that when you were playing for him, but then you realize that's not right because you had to have that certain level of respect. He wasn't your friend. He was your coach, but when you left, he was your friend."

Olson made it clear when you were in school you were a student-athlete and no friend. Elliott recalled having to go to a luncheon with Olson before practice one day. It was his junior year, and Arizona was the talk of the town. "We spoke at the event together," Elliott recalled. "When we were driving back before practice, he asked if I had eaten, and I hadn't yet. He pulled out $20, and back then that $20 could have been $1,000. I had no money. So, in the back of my mind, I was thinking how I could get McDonald's, get a couple cheeseburgers, and a drink. And then I was gonna save the rest of the money for the week. But when he gave me the money, he said, 'Bring me my receipt and my change.' I was flabbergasted. I'm thinking, *You can't give me $17?* He was just so straight and even-keeled like that. I wouldn't say he was miserly; he would just do things by the rules."

Olson was a man of integrity, someone who wouldn't bend those NCAA rules to give extra money to a player. It's one of the reasons Elliott and others think of him so highly. "Only a few people in my inner circle know this: I'm going back to school. I've been taking classes online and I only have four classes left and I'm done," Elliott said. "And the reason I'm doing that is because of Coach Olson and my mom. I promised them both I'd finish."

Graduating will be his final thank you to Olson for supporting him all these years. "I see all the pictures around my house and I miss him a bunch, a ton," Elliott said. "I just miss hearing his voice because he was a gentle person. I miss my conversations with him. I could feel the happiness in his voice when we talked…He'll always be a part of me."

2 Steve Kerr

Whether it was a phone call from his father, Malcolm; the admiration for Lute Olson by his mother; or a great showing in front of Olson during a made-for-scholarship moment, it seems Steve Kerr and the University of Arizona were destined to be together. "Serendipitous," Kerr said. "It was pretty fortuitous that it worked out."

Back in Pacific Palisades, California, where Kerr lived with his family, former Duke star and current San Antonio Spurs assistant coach Chip Engelland set up a practice with a few players from the area to show Olson what Kerr could do. At the time, Kerr was lightly recruited and wanted to play college basketball. "He pulled all the guys aside before Lute got there and said, 'Coach Olson's coming to see Steve play,'" Kerr said. "'I want to make sure everybody knows what's happening, so if you're going to close out on Steve, that's fine but don't block his shot. You can make it look like you're playing defense but make sure he gets his shots off. We want him to get the scholarship.' There was a reason why I hadn't been recruited. I wasn't very athletic."

That practice organized by Engelland occurred in the summer of 1983 when Arizona's Olson, who had just months before become the school's head coach, was looking to fill out his roster.

He was late in the recruiting game and needed players. It's been well-documented that Kerr's mom had admired Olson from afar, saying he was the kind of coach she'd love to have him play for after previously hearing him speak at a luncheon. And, well, he was "so handsome, too." But it was a call from Kerr's father to Olson that really sealed the deal. "He was kind of the key to the whole thing," Kerr said. "Coach Olson didn't actually offer me a scholarship. He called me and told me he was interested, and then I didn't hear from him. While that was happening, Cal State Fullerton offered me a scholarship. I was waiting to hear from Coach Olson because he had said he was going to call me back, and he didn't. During that time I told Cal State Fullerton I was going to go there. My dad then asked me where I wanted to go. I told him Arizona. So, he said he'd call Coach Olson to see what was going on. I thought that was great."

Malcolm tracked him down and found out that, indeed, there was still a scholarship, and it was available. He made it happen. "My dad loved [Olson]," Kerr said. "He knew that was the place to be and knew where I wanted to be and where I should be—based on Coach Olson and the school. He visited in October of my freshman year and visited with Coach Olson. We went to a football game, and he came to a practice. It was fun for him to visit the campus and meet the new coach."

So, Kerr was officially a student-athlete, and the aura about Olson started. "We were all intimidated by him," Kerr said. "He was scary and such a dominant presence. And obviously his reputation preceded him. He was a great coach. I think we're all nervous to be around him."

Still, few had the relationship with Olson that Kerr did. They became closer when Kerr's father was assassinated in 1984 in Beirut. Malcolm was the president of American University in Beirut at the time. "When my dad died, I spent a weekend at his house, and that's when our relationship changed pretty dramatically," he said. "The Olsons really took care of me. They did that before, too. They felt a responsibility for me."

When Olson talked about family, it included his family and the players. "We were all a family," Kerr said. "They wanted everybody to feel part of the family, but I think they felt an extra responsibility for me."

Steve Kerr (Courtesy Matt Othick)

That weekend Kerr stayed with them, Lute's wife, Bobbi, handed Kerr a beer while he was relaxing in the family's jacuzzi. "I was in there and so was his son, Steve, and Lute was not out there," he said. "Bobbi handed us each a beer and said, 'Don't let Lute know.' Typical Bobbi. He didn't know."

And so the relationship grew and thrived with Kerr being so close to Olson on so many levels. It didn't hurt that Arizona got to the NCAA Tournament in Olson's second year. And then again in his third year and then fourth year. It was clearly the start of something special.

Then came the summer of 1986 when Kerr, while playing for the United States' national team, suffered a severe knee injury and had to sit out the entire 1986–87 season. "Everything that happened solidified our relationship," Kerr said. "We were already successful, and I had played for the national team he was coaching. But I was able to spend an extra year on campus red-shirting. We definitely grew closer."

Olson was rarely a "touchy, feely-get-close type," said Kerr, who called it a "generational thing," though he still found a way to get through. He also said the team helped form a connection by being really good in 1987–88 when Arizona made its first serious run in the tournament to reach its first Final Four. "It was the whole group that inspired him...and vice versa," he said. "There was really a feel of family by then. And we had a dynamic group of guys, like Tom Tolbert and Sean Elliott, [Matt] Muehlebach...The guys were great, and everything clicked. Coach was really enjoying himself. The first couple of years, he was under a lot of stress to rebound the program. By then, it was really thriving. That was probably the happiest I had ever seen him during my last couple of years in school."

Kerr was so comfortable with Olson that he could joke about him on a radio show. "I was obviously making a stupid joke," Kerr said, laughing. "Someone asked me about having a New Year's resolution, and I said a wise-ass comment that my resolution was to help Coach O kick his heroin habit. I'm not sure how he felt, but obviously I knew at that point it was easy to kind of mess around like that and get away with it. But I wouldn't have said that my first few years."

Arizona fell to Oklahoma in the semifinals at the 1988 Final Four, and Kerr shot 2-for-13. He remembers it often, he has said. Arizona returned home to a parade and a large gathering at Arizona Stadium. After a few words of wisdom from a few people, Olson found it so comfortable he started dancing on the stage. The crowd roared, and his players laughed and lived it up. "That's how fun that season was and how relaxed he was," Kerr said. "That was as happy as I had ever seen him as well. He loved that team. And he had a great recruiting class coming in and he knew the program was headed in the right direction. He was in his prime. He was legitimately having a good time."

Then off Kerr went to have what eventually turned into an illustrious NBA career, winning five NBA titles as a player and three as an NBA head coach. He was a lead analyst for TNT and later for Turner and CBS who announced the NCAA Tournament. He's been the head coach of the Golden State Warriors since 2014. All the while he stayed connected with his former coach. "We obviously stayed in touch and we probably talked once a month or so," Kerr said. "If UA was in the same area I was in, I'd go over to see him. I then bought a house in Tucson in my early NBA years, so we'd spend time in the summer, going to dinner with him and Bobbi. I'd speak at his camps or just go by his office. So we stayed really close."

Before cellphones were commonplace, Olson was usually the first to congratulate him. "He was always good about staying in touch," Kerr said.

And Kerr was there for him as often as he could be. Kerr, who was then playing with the San Antonio Spurs, was at the Elite Eight game when Arizona beat Illinois in San Antonio in 2001. "I remember driving from the airport after a road trip and celebrating with Coach. The same happened in Indianapolis when they won the whole thing. Jud Buechler and our wives drove down to watch that game. We were always connected to the program."

No one could have been prouder of Olson than Kerr when Arizona won the title in 1997 after beating Kentucky in overtime. "No question, we were so happy for him," he said. "Remember that he was coming off a string of early losses in the tournament. He had been taking heat nationally and locally because their expectations were so high. It was so fun to see him break through."

Kerr was there for Olson, and Olson was there for Kerr. Olson was there in the front row at the press conference when Kerr was named the head coach of the Warriors in 2014 and again when he was named the Coach of the Year in 2016. When he was announced as the new head coach with the Warriors, Kerr, who had not previously been a coach at any level, said Arizona was where he saw how to grow a program. "I learned an awful lot about consistency of effort, of preparation, consistency of the message that he provided for the players," Kerr said. "I was part of that growth and process. That's something I will never forget."

He was in awe of Olson then and he will always continue to be, which Kerr revealed at Olson's Celebration of Life in the fall of 2021. "[He] changed the entire course of my life, and I'd say the same thing about people here," he said. "And ultimately, that's his greatest accomplishment: bringing us all together and creating this family...He was a great culture builder. Everything that he taught, I was just absorbing everything. It was a master's class in leadership and coaching and family and community. Everything that I learned [at Arizona] has translated to my entire life and everything that I've done—from raising a family to coaching teams to being a part of the community. We did all of that here."

Kerr described his appreciation for his former coach during that Celebration of Life ceremony. "It was nice to have that relationship and to always have his support," he said. "He's a Hall of Fame coach and so respected, so to have his support and have him there for me, it meant a lot. I think in a lot of ways—playing for him and having his support—validated me in many ways and gave me credibility. That was where my career in basketball began because of his influence not only in giving me a chance at Arizona, but continuing with his support through the years."

Kerr offered some final reflections. "I definitely miss him," he said. "He had such an amazing presence even until the end when I would see him. There was part of me that was kind of reverential. He just had that kind of presence. He was a commanding figure, and every time I saw him, I'd be thrilled to see him but slightly nervous. That's what he meant to me, in fact, to all of us."

3
Mike
Bibby

Mike Bibby may have been one of the best players Lute Olson ever recruited. He was an in-state kid and would end up as Arizona's all-time best prep scorer. He led the state with 3,002 points out of Shadow Mountain, where he won a state title and eventually brought those talents to Arizona. He's still one of the best players—and natives—at Arizona, eventually choosing the program over Duke and UCLA. "Being close to home was part of it," he said. "Bobbi Olson was a big part of it. Coach Olson was a big part of me coming to the school...I had watched them since the ninth or 10th grade. I saw them in the NCAA Tournament, just seeing them play in it, but they lost in the first rounds. A lot of people were telling me, 'Hey, the team loses a lot in the first round. Why would you go there?' I told them, 'We're not going to lose in the first round when I get there.' That was that was the main thing. It was a big deal going to Arizona, being close to home. The main thing was playing for Coach Olson. He'd let teams play to their strengths and to the player's strengths."

Olson called Bibby "a tremendous competitor" while he was at the University of Arizona.

"I remember Coach coming in my house the first time when I committed," Bibby said. "It was him and coach [Jessie] Evans coming in, and he had the biggest smile. I remember it like it was yesterday."

Of course, Olson wore a suit during that memorable visit. "He was always in a suit," Bibby said, laughing. "And my mom loved him. My mom felt good in sending me there to Arizona. When you send your kid off to college, you're not going to feel comfortable with the coach unless they do the best for your son or daughter, and she felt that way about him."

With Bibby's mom on board, Arizona was the call. Olson can also thank the history of the program he built and the reputation he had with point guards. Back then, Point Guard U—Arizona's moniker at the time—was well established behind the likes of Khalid Reeves, Damon Stoudamire, Steve Kerr, and others. "They were good players," Bibby said. "He let them play basketball, and that's what intrigued me. I knew he was a great coach and what he did for his team and point guards was exactly what I needed and what I wanted. And what I wanted was to be in the NBA. And that school put out a lot of NBA point guards and good ones. So, I knew it was the right spot of where I wanted to be. And everything he did with me was great."

Arizona was coming off a Sweet 16 appearance in 1996, but it had lost its whole starting lineup, returning only Miles Simon and Michael Dickerson. And Arizona needed a point guard. Bibby was the perfect fit. "The team was already established, and coming in I just wanted to fit in," he said. "I didn't want to ruffle any feathers. I didn't want to step on toes. I just kind of played to fit in my freshman year."

And play he did. He fit in like he had been part of the program for a while. He had the senses and wherewithal of a cagey veteran.

He also had the chance to shine while Simon was out because of academic issues. So, behind Bibby, Dickerson, Bennett Davison, A.J. Bramlett, Gene Edgerson, and others, UA flourished.

Eventually, Simon came back at the beginning of the second semester, taking some time to get back in the groove with the others. Arizona finished fifth in the Pac-10 Conference, getting a No. 4 seed in the NCAA Tournament. That's when Arizona took off. In fact, that's when Bibby *really* took off. "I remember in the tournament he sat me down, and it was a team meeting, and he told me, 'Mike, I need you to be more aggressive,'" Bibby said. "That's when I opened up more, and I started being more aggressive. I started taking more shots. It was the best thing I think to have happen in my career."

His coach believed in him, and Bibby believed even more in himself. And this is from a player who had this reputation of being a flashy player in high school. It was thought he'd be that way, too, when he arrived at Arizona. "I was that guy in high school, but it's a lot easier to do that stuff in high school," he said.

So, did Olson say he couldn't do that while at Arizona? "No, he never told me not to do anything," Bibby said. "That was what made him such a great coach. He never told players not to do anything. You get a lot of that nowadays. My son was on a team, and their coach told them that you're not allowed to dribble in the paint and you're not allowed to take more than two dribbles when you get the ball. You're not allowed to do anything but shoot jumpers. When you put restrictions on kids like that, you're not going to get the best out of them. And I think that's what made Coach Olson such a player's coach: he let us play to our strengths. He allowed us to get out and run and play basketball. That's what made us so good."

If anything, it was Bibby himself who put the restrictions on his play because it was important that he mesh with his older teammates. "It wasn't really restrictions. It was just not stepping on any toes and to fit in," he said. "There was like four or five freshmen that came in. I think I might have been the only person that got significant time. The team was set and good. I wanted to come in and play to them. Instead of me going out and trying to be the star, I wanted to play to them. It was about fitting in."

More importantly, Bibby never felt intimidated by Olson, even though he had this towering presence. "He never had that cocky attitude ever," he said. "He was the nicest man in the world. He genuinely cared about us. You don't have that in a lot of coaches today, ones that genuinely care about their players."

Bibby said Olson never put pressure on him to perform, especially at a time when Arizona was one of the best teams in the country. "That's what made it so easy to go out there and play because I can say he didn't put any pressure," he said. "It wasn't a case of if I made a mistake, I'd come out the game. You see a lot of coaches do that: make a mistake and you come out. You can't play like that. I made a lot of mistakes when I played, but I was never taken out for making those mistakes. And that's what helped me grow."

Olson had the reputation of being a strait-laced guy. Though that had some truth, he would also reveal his personality. "He'd crack jokes here and there, but, yes, he was more stoic," Bibby said. "He was a very serious man, but you could tell he cared. It wasn't intimidating, and that made it a lot easier."

Bibby flourished under Olson's guidance. "He just kind of let me run the team," he said. "He let me go out there and do what I did my whole life. That's what made it so easy for me to take that next step."

It's a reason why there was no better situation than UA—especially because of its location. "It was just an hour and a half away from home. I was going home every weekend," he said.

Mike Bibby (Courtesy Mike Bibby)

"My mom would do my laundry. I'd take her all my laundry on Friday and bring it back on Sunday. She'd send food for everybody. My mom cooked food for everybody. So, it was it was a perfect place for me to be."

And if his mother wasn't doing all she could—for the team and Bibby—Bobbi was doing her part, too. It's been well-chronicled she was the perfect team mom. "She was the mother figure... and I'm a momma's boy," Bibby said. "She knew that coming in and she said she'd take care of me. It was a big deal for me for her to be there and be a part of that."

And Olson was a father figure. "He was like a gentle giant kind of guy," he said. "Everybody loved him. There was nothing that he could ever get wrong or could ever do wrong...Him taking me under his wing and showing me the ropes without being too harsh was perfect."

Olson was also the ideal buffer for Mike when Arizona would face USC and Bibby's father, Henry. At the time Mike and Henry were estranged. Olson would deflect the news to make it be more about Arizona and USC, never about Bibby vs. Bibby. "I kind of remember him doing that, but that was good," he said. "I wasn't a great or a big-time talker or media person talking like that. It was tough for me to even be in that situation and to play at the level I was playing at."

Arizona eventually got to the pinnacle in Mike Bibby's first season, winning the title in overtime against Kentucky. He had become the first true freshman guard to help his team win an NCAA title. How did Olson act after the game? "He was the same," he said. "There was no funny business. We had a lot of jokes on the team and had a lot of fun and got along. He was the same guy. It was great for him to get that because he deserved it. He deserved many more. But I'm glad he got that one. I was glad to be part of it."

Then came Arizona's run at a repeat title. UA went 17–1 in the Pac-10, losing to Henry Bibby's USC team on a fluke-ish type shot that hit the back of the rim with a thud and fell in. Eventually, Arizona was the No. 1 team in the West and lost to Utah in the Elite Eight. "Repeating is one of the hardest things to do," Bibby said. "We weren't supposed to win it the first year, but it was the second year. We lost that game to USC, but we expected to win it again. It was unfortunate we had a bad shooting night against Utah."

Before that drive to repeat, Arizona took a trip to Australia, one that was already scheduled before the 1997 title run. Initially, it was thought that 1998 would be the year Arizona would have that special run. But it came a little more than a month after UA had won the title, and no Wildcats player wanted to be there. They wanted to rest. So while in Australia, the team gathered in a hotel room to talk about getting unified to talk to Coach about going home. They had had enough of Australia. "We said, 'Let's let him know we're not taking no for an answer,'" Bibby said, laughing. "We went to him, and the first thing he said was, 'That's not going to happen.' He shot us down right from the start. But I thought it was a good bonding situation for the guys, even though no one really wanted to be there. I ate at McDonald's for however many days we were there, every meal. It wasn't fun. But we did go in the ocean. It was cool. But we just didn't want to be there. But when you look back at it now, you're thankful for that situation."

Then Arizona got ready to pursue a back-to-back title—before ultimately getting upset by Utah. "He might have been more relaxed," he said. "I think he felt we were, too. It just turned out it was a bad night, and in college basketball, you can't have that."

Shortly after the loss to Utah, Bibby made the decision public—one that everyone already suspected—that he'd leave for a chance at the NBA. "He knew it was coming," Bibby said. "I went up to him and told him I was going to do what's best for my family, and he understood. In fact, he kind of pushed me a little bit to go. I didn't need pushing, but he respected whatever my decision was."

Bibby went on to become the second overall pick of the 1998 draft, the highest for a former Arizona player at the time. He enjoyed a long career in the NBA. Bibby credits Olson. "He's the one guy who made me the player that I am and got me to that next level," he said. "He made me feel comfortable. And gave me the confidence I needed to make it happen."

Bibby's jersey was later retired at UA. "It was great to be part of that at an arena that bears his name," he said. "To have my name up there in the rafters is an amazing feeling."

Bibby learned a lot from Olson. While winning a number of high school titles and looking to get into coaching at the college or pro level, Bibby has adopted his former college coach's style. "It's about letting kids play and not [getting worked up] when kids make a mistake, as long as they play hard," he said. "A lot of the confidence he gave me, I gave to these kids. As long as you play hard, you can play for me."

4
Damon Stoudamire

Damon Stoudamire—all 5'10" of him—was truly "Mighty Mouse," a nickname given to him because of his power on the court. He was fantastic in four years at Arizona, finishing as an All-American and as part of one of Arizona's all-time backcourts with Khalid Reeves. "I came to Arizona because I knew if I did, Coach O would make be a better basketball player," Stoudamire said. "And I wanted to win."

He did often.

In addition to winning, there was growing. And, well, growing up. "I'd never met a coach who had a plan for everybody," Stoudamire said.

Lute Olson had a plan, though not everyone bought into it. "I still talk to Sean Allen," Stoudamire said of his former roommate at UA in the early 1990s. "He lives overseas after playing over there. To this day, he said the biggest mistake he made was not listening to Coach Olson. He just thought he was a know-it-all. Like I told him, 'Man, what do we know? We were kids.' Hindsight is 20/20, and Arizona isn't for everybody."

Even some of the ones who stayed thought about leaving. Former UA player Ray Owes was one of those players. "Ray packed up his truck and drove all the way back to San Bernardino, California," Stoudamire said. "These are stories people don't know. He said, 'I'm out' and that he was going to transfer and not come back. Ray was miserable as a freshman. He went home every weekend when he could. Coach got on a plane and got him."

And Owes returned. Stoudamire praised how "genuine" Olson was and said that the players who departed might have made impulsive decisions. "I felt anybody that left or transferred early was because of a lack of patience," he said. "He had a plan for everybody. He had a plan for Damon Stoudamire. He had a plan for Ray Owes."

What Stoudamire admired most was Olson's honesty with his players. "I always loved him because of that," he said. "I had four schools that told me I was going to come in and start as a freshman. Coach Olson was the only one who told me I was gonna have to work. And, obviously, I didn't start right away. That wasn't even a question."

Olson made it clear that Reeves was returning (after coming off the bench) and that Matt Othick was there, too. Arizona had a strong team, coming off a Sweet 16 in 1991. "He said I was capable of playing," Stoudamire said, "but again that I'd have to work."

Olson had seen what Stoudamire was capable of as a high school sophomore in Las Vegas during recruiting season. "You know Coach O," Stoudamire said, "he gives you that nod to let you know he's interested. He later told my coaches that he loved my speed and quickness and how I changed the game with my pace, things of that nature."

Olson had to worry about Oregon and then Louisville in pursuit. In fact, Louisville made a last-second push to get

Damon Stoudamire in the
1994 Final Four (AP Images)

Stoudamire. The coaches found out about it. "Coach Tony McAndrews and I were talking about that recently," Stoudamire said. "We laughed. He remembered telling Coach Olson that Louisville was making that push and that maybe they'd lose me. Man, that next day they were in Portland. I remember like it was yesterday. They met me at my high school. They must have been on an early flight or something."

Of course, Stoudamire chose Arizona in part because he was drawn to Olson, who had such a presence. "I've never seen a man control the room like he did," Stoudamire said. "When he walked into a gym, people knew he walked into the gym. I'm not sure there was a coach in the country who commanded the respect that he did in that gym. The only coach to get that—and it's crazy to even think about it—but it was Coach Olson and Jerry Tarkanian. They were by far the two biggest guys. When they walked into the gym, they had a following. If Arizona or UNLV was recruiting you, you had made it."

Stoudamire had a memorable first visit to Tucson, and Olson led the way. "The man had so much charisma," he said. "I remember him picking me up at the airport, and he came in his Lexus. I get into his car and I'm thinking: *The only people I knew who had Lexus cars were drug dealers.* I had never seen a legit guy drive a Lexus. He hit a button, and it started up. I'll never forget that. I'm sitting in the car, and it was intimidating but not in a bad way. He just commanded the room. To this day, I've never been around a guy that commanded a room like he did. He had big hands, he was a big guy, was a handsome guy, a sharp dresser. He was well put together. You know he really had that whole thing down."

There was that mutual respect, as well. Stoudamire and Olson always had a great relationship. Olson knew early Stoudamire would bring success to the program, and Olson would bring success to Stoudamire. "From the first time I stepped onto the campus, my teammates will probably say this too: I was a teacher's pet. I could do no wrong," he said. "But what people don't understand is with that came a lot of responsibility. We had a lot of conversations about different things. And he put a lot on me."

Stoudamire said the responsibility really ramped up his sophomore year when Arizona faced USC and UCLA on the road early in the Pac-10 season. That weekend Stoudamire remembered getting more than 25 assists with only a turnover in two games. "I gained his trust then," he said. "I remember him saying in an article that I was irreplaceable and that I set the tone for us. From that point forward, those statements gave me confidence. After that, I'd go in and talk to him about my thoughts on different things. We had that rapport, and I'm not sure anybody else had that with him. But we had that."

Of course, there were times—many times—he was tough on Stoudamire. After all, he was the leader. "I can remember the Texas Tech game [in the Fiesta Bowl Classic], and a couple of things happened. I came down on somebody's ankle. I made it through the game. The next day my ankle was killing me. I'm going around hobbled a bit and I'm thinking I'll be able to take it easy. [Trainer Steve] Condo looked at it and worked on it. And Coach comes around and asks, 'What's this?' I say my ankle is messed up. He got a stationary bike for me, and I'm thinking that was just a bunch of BS. So, I'm thinking I'm going to do a Sunday stroll on it. He came over there and put everything up for high speed. Man, he had me in a full-blown sweat. Here my ankle was as big as an orange. But I look back on those coaching moments, and at the end of the day, your best players want to be coached anyway."

Olson pushed Stoudamire to get the best out of his point guard. "He never challenged me publicly," Stoudamire said. "But I was pretty consistent with him. He would behind closed doors. If something happened or if something was not right, he'd get after me. I was fine with it because I knew everything he was telling me was going to make me better."

That was the case, as well, when Stoudamire was suspended for the final game of his career after reports that his father, Willie, received a plane ticket from an agent unbeknownst to Damon. "Everything was good," Damon said of Olson's reaction back then. "Coach always had my back. That was always the case with people from Arizona. But he was okay with it."

It's not like they didn't have disagreements. One big one came while his career was over, and Bryan Colangelo of the Phoenix Suns called to invite him to play in the Desert Classic, an All-Star gathering for NBA prospects. Stoudamire declined the invitation, feeling he was already going to be a high draft choice. "Coach was mad because he felt I needed to do it," he said. "I told him I didn't need to play in it, that I've shown these NBA people what I can do for four years."

Olson told Stoudamire that he was wrong and needed to do it. He asked him why he thought he didn't need to go. Stoudamire said the discussion got heated. "Number one, I played for you. You're regarded as one of the top coaches for making his players ready for the NBA, and that's a fact," Stoudamire told him.

"Number two, I was All-Freshman team. Number three, I was a three-time All-Pac-10 Team. Number four, I was Co-Player of the Year with UCLA's Ed O'Bannon. Five, I was first-team consensus All-American. Six, I played USA Basketball, playing in the Olympic Festival, the World Games, the Goodwill Games, and I played against the Dream Team."

Olson still didn't agree. "Then, I said, I played against a dude [Reeves] who went in the lottery last season," Stoudamire said. "I went against him every day."

Still not agreeing with him, Olson got on the phone with 10 NBA executives—with Stoudamire in the room and the phone on speaker—and asked them about his point guard. "Each one of them said Damon was going to be the first guard taken in the draft," Stoudamire said, "that I didn't have to go to the Desert Classic."

It was the first time Stoudamire had won an argument against Olson. "And the only time," he said.

Stoudamire became the No. 7 overall pick of the 1995 NBA Draft and was named the league's Rookie of the Year.

In his post-Arizona life, they often talked. "Coach was all about family," he said. "It was like he was like the Godfather tying everybody together. He wanted his guys to come back, come visit with him. He always kept up with what the guys were up to. He'd come up and watch me play when I was with Portland, and we'd play in Phoenix. He'd come up and see me, Steve Kerr, and Sean Elliott when they were with San Antonio. It was him. He kept everything going. He was so good at that stuff."

He'd still call Stoudamire's mom to check in on her. She'd go to the Oregon and Oregon State games when Arizona played them in the Stoudamires' native state. "She loves him," he said. "He was always good with those things."

More importantly, Olson always had time for his guys. In the last few years, as Olson got older, Stoudamire would fly in for a quick visit. "We'd just reminisce," he said. "He was getting older. But one thing about that man [as is the case as you get older], he might not have remembered what happened three days ago, but he remembered what happened in practice in the fall of 1993. What I saw near the end was he loved talking about basketball. It lit him up, just lit him up. It was therapeutic for both of us."

Stoudamire misses him. Few players were closer to Olson. "I looked at him as a mentor/father," he said. "He never ever preached. He was never outwardly with advice, but he led by actions, and that was every day. He led by example. People say grind it out and do this and that, but he practiced it every day. He was a great man."

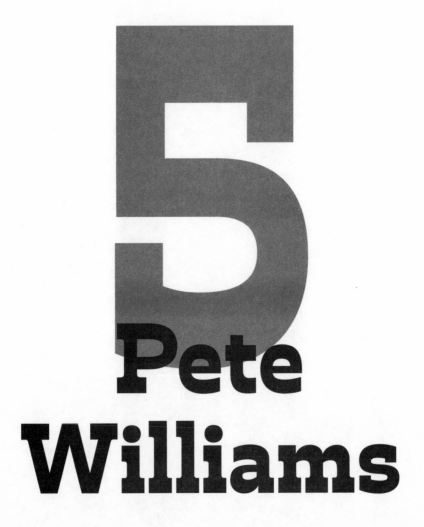

5

Pete
Williams

ete Williams is often called the "Cornerstone" of the Arizona program under Lute Olson. He was a big reason why UA was able to find some success early and why eventually the program took off. Yes, Williams was that important to the program, even though he was a late-signing recruit out of junior college.

It's likely he had more information on Olson—at the time—than anyone in the program. He had followed his career at Iowa. "When he took the job at Arizona in spring of '83, I was, like so many other people, stunned, shocked, you name it," Williams said. "Why would you leave Iowa to a downgrade program like Arizona at that time?"

Williams had been recruited by TCU, Colorado, and UNLV. Olson had asked a West Coast coach about who were the best players who had yet to sign. Williams' name came up. So Olson reached out to Williams and decided to visit him at his junior college. By then the regular season was over, and the guys would just have scrimmages with one another. Olson showed up to the scrimmage. "I don't care what anyone says, but Coach even back then had the steps," Williams said. "Man, that was something else. The fact that I was well aware of his background, especially that 1979–80 season with Iowa going to the Final Four, and now he was on campus to see me [was crazy]. I was blown away. As it turned out, I played pretty well that morning. It could have been nerve-wracking, and I could have played badly, and he could have said, 'Nah, we don't want him,' but I played well. So we set up a recruiting trip…and the rest is history."

Williams flew in and met Scott Thompson and others, and they caravanned with other recruits and drove to UA. "Remember, this is 1983. There was little development out there and there was a dust storm on the way back," Williams said. "I said, 'Wow, looks like we're on a mission to rebuild the program.' Coach Thompson looked at me and said, 'That's exactly what we're gonna do.' It was just the way everything played out. It's just been mindboggling to me."

Williams committed right then, which started a player-coach relationship and ultimately a friend-coach relationship. "It takes a while to build that up," Williams said. "And a lot of things go into play. Number one, your effort on the court, off the court, in the classroom, in the community, being a good teammate, someone who's going to work hard and everything, and it's understood. I think I earned a little more respect based on the work I put in. I was undersized [at 6'9" playing the center position] and tasked with physical disadvantages going against other people. I never let that stop me from working hard and knowing that Coach Olson was one who didn't accept excuses. I had no choice but to work hard."

In the early months, practices were tough, and the drills were unusual. Olson made them jump rope many times. "And I hate to jump rope," Williams said. "Hate it."

But when Olson said do something, you did it. "It was intimidating but in a really respectful way, not in a scary way," Williams said. "There were times we'd be shooting around getting ready and getting loose. But as soon as Coach made his presence in the gym…it was all business, all business. He was just such an impressive man. I'll go as far to say I was in awe of him. I still am. His physical stature, he was just built strong, looked nice, and was intelligent, knew everything about life and basketball, and the whole nine. I was in awe of him."

Some former players have said playing for Olson was like playing for their grandfather. For Williams it was a bit different. "Everybody had their different perspective, but for me it was playing for someone you truly respect, and I'll put love into the equation," Williams said. "Because as time went on, the love was on a whole other level. [But that was later in life.] But as a coach at the time, you really appreciate and respect him more than anything. Once you get out of school, and life goes on, you really start realizing all the things that he was doing back then was to help you become a better player and a better person in life."

There were some Arizona players who didn't truly appreciate Olson until later in life when they had time to reflect, but Williams welcomed his help even at the time. "Yeah, I did," he said, "because I was always used to working hard."

The early part was rough going. Arizona lost seven of its first nine games and 11 of its first 14. But the games were close, very close. Sometimes one-possession games. There was one game early in Olson's career at UA when Williams saw Olson lose it. It was eye-opening. Arizona had just lost its fourth game—to Pan American, no less—at home. "Bobbi once told me, 'Lute isn't a yeller or a screamer,'" Williams said in Bobbi's voice for effect. "'When he gets upset, all he'll do is give you is that look [of disappointment].' But there he was yelling and screaming in the locker room. He had a clipboard; he went off. He told us, 'Now I see why you were a bunch of losers last year' and then threw the clipboard, and it whizzed by my head. The first thing that came to mind was: *Wait a minute, Bobbi said he didn't yell or scream.*"

Things got better, and some were close games, but that didn't serve as consolation. "Coach O didn't like moral victories," Williams said. "The culture was so bad—rock bottom—so he had to come in and change that...As a group collectively, you can say that maybe, maybe we were okay. The fact that we kept things close and we were that little train that could [was

Pete Williams (Courtesy Andy Morales)

refreshing] because we fought hard and were in every game. But that wasn't enough for him. He wouldn't be as successful as he is, or was, if he accepted moral victories. This whole thing is we have to win and eventually learn how. So it was tough, but I knew it would all be good for us in the long run."

Arizona had found its stride and finished strong, going 6–2 down the stretch while beating Oregon, Oregon State, USC, Stanford, Arizona State, and Washington State. "We didn't want the season to end," he said. "We were hoping that maybe, just maybe, the NIT might give us a little consideration because of the way we finished, but that didn't happen. We were just really disappointed the season had to end."

Olson knew he had something. Arizona returned a majority of its top players, and recruiting was taking off. "People don't know, but had Richard Hollis stayed at Arizona—he would have been a freshman my senior year—who knows?" Williams said. "He was the most talented player that had come to the program. He just didn't make it. And if Mike [Tait] doesn't [transfer], we have something that could have been special."

Arizona still made it to the NCAA Tournament in the second year. "But I still think it could have been so much more fun," Williams said.

It was less fun when Olson sent Williams home after not making curfew on a road trip, a crucial road trip, no less. It was late into the year in 1985 in Seattle, and Williams and Morgan Taylor stayed out after a grueling 60–58 loss to Washington. At the time, Arizona was close to clinching its first Pac-10 men's basketball title. But Olson sent Williams and Taylor home before its crucial game with UCLA, a game it lost 58–54, and that ended

UA's hopes of a Pac-10 title. In a team meeting, Olson showed how upset he was with his senior leader. "Not even looking at me," Williams said, "that showed how disappointed he was in me."

Williams has spoken about it so many times that he's used it as an example to those he deals with as a probation officer in the Los Angeles area. He's called it a "black spot" on his career but a "learning one." "I've gone on the record to say it's my whole foundation, my whole being, and what I am now as a parent," he said. "Me being a father and how I project myself is a direct reflection of Lute. It was a brain-freeze moment, which was totally out of character for me. It really hit home because we had a chance to explain our actions. Each individual player spoke to it, and he looked at them dead in the eye. I was the last one to speak, and as soon as I spoke, he looked at the floor. He wouldn't look at me. That crushed me more than you could ever believe. You know to this day it still hurts. But what I really appreciate is how we were able to balance our relationship and grow even stronger. I went on his radio show. I accepted my responsibility. It was a learning experience. To this day, I'm so obsessed with doing things the right way because I don't want there ever be a time where coaches will say they are ashamed of my actions, and a lot of that stems from the learning experience I had back then. I know that will never happen again."

Arizona made the tournament but lost in the first round. The future was bright. "He was pleased because I don't know if anybody saw us getting to the tournament in two years," Williams said. "He was excited about the opportunity of getting to the tournament but disappointed with the end result. Coach O was all about winning."

Williams was later drafted by the Denver Nuggets in the second round—and made the team. "Our relationship grew to another level from there," Williams said.

At the time Williams had officially made the team, Denver set up a scrimmage to show off the squad to the fans. It was a meet-the-team get-together. Williams, of course, played well in the scrimmage, showing Denver it wasn't wrong in keeping him. "After the scrimmage we are all there signing autographs," Williams said. "And out of the blue, I hear a voice in line say, 'Can I be next?' I recognized the voice and look up. Standing right in front of me was Coach O with a big ol' smile. I had no clue he'd be there. Not sure how he knew to be there. Maybe he knew I'd made the team before I did or he was just passing through and decided to see me. Whatever the case, he was there. That meant the world to me…We went out, we had dinner together. I believe that might have been the first time he and I had a one-on-one. It was just beautiful, man…We're Arizona basketball, and you're part of the family. Coach was always big on family. I can't speak to other programs, but when it came to Arizona, it was that in every sense of the word."

Olson kept in touch often. One time Arizona was facing UCLA and USC, and he asked if Williams' son, Mark, would like to be a ball boy. Of course, the answer was yes. "He'd be out there getting the balls or giving them water," Williams said. "It totally blew my mind. He got a chance to go to the locker room at halftime and hear his wrath. Arizona was getting beat at halftime. I asked Mark, 'What did he say?' 'I don't know, but he was doing a bunch of yelling.'"

There was a time when in the summer of 1984—before Williams' senior year—Olson sent him a card from Taiwan to say hello and to make sure he was putting in the work for his final season. "Hope you're working hard on the weights and your endurance, as well as playing a lot," Olson wrote. "See you in a couple of weeks…"

The letter had the desired impact. "I just thought this was so cool," Williams said. "I was doing everything except the weights. But he made it clear and in no uncertain terms I needed to be in the best shape. He knew I could do so much more [my senior year]."

Years later—in a game played in front of thousands at McKale Center—former UA players returned for a reunion of sorts. Nearly 20 years after leaving UA, Williams returned and looked like he could still suit up and play with the current players. "He was like a proud father seeing all his sons coming back," Williams said. "I loved it when he gave me some praise, saying even at 40-something I was still the best player on the court. I was low-key about it, but don't get me wrong: I loved it."

Williams not only thought he was part of a family at Arizona, but also still values lessons he learned from Olson. "While you're playing, you're still young and you have a respect for your coach, and that's that," Williams said. "But the love rises when you get out because you see what everything he tried to teach you and what it all means. It was those random phone calls of me calling him or him calling me. There were many discussions about many things, but the advice that stuck the most for me was: good people find a way to be successful. Surround yourself with good people, and good things will happen. Negative people have a way of bringing the foundation down. I look at my history, my crew [of friends], my high school boys where we've been together since 1981, and there is not a knucklehead in the bunch. Whatever direction you choose to go in, surround yourself with good people. Another one is there's never an excuse for not being able to work hard. It's that simple."

Those life lessons from his coach still apply. Williams said he misses Olson "dearly." "The fact that I can't pick up the phone and call him—or him calling me—is different," Williams said.

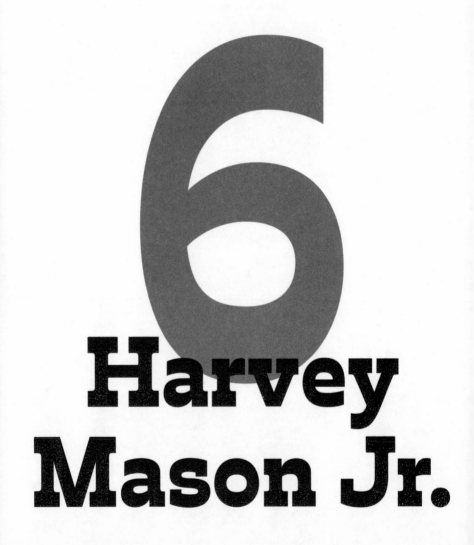

6
Harvey
Mason Jr.

iven the background of Harvey Mason Jr., whose father was a jazz drummer, record producer, and member of the band Fourplay, he met some big names in the music business while growing up. So one might think meeting Lute Olson would be just another day. It wasn't. "It was a huge deal," Harvey Mason Jr. said. "It was because playing basketball was a dream. I wanted to be a college basketball player and had fantasies of being a professional basketball player one day. So meeting Coach Olson was a step toward what I thought was one of my life's goals. I remember he came in our living room. My mom pretty much melted. And my dad really liked him. He was huge, by the way. I don't know why, but when he came into our living room, he was immense. He was tall, he was wide, and his hands were big. He was impressive. He said all the right things in my living room. I was sold."

Mason Jr. went to Arizona because of Olson. The program hadn't really been established yet, though you could see that it was headed in the right direction. He committed as a junior in high school in the mid-1980s. "It was because of Coach Olson and the talent he had recruited," he said. "My recruiting hosts were Sean Elliott and Anthony Cook. They were freshmen. I went to practices and saw how amazing they were. I saw Kenny

Lofton, saw Steve Kerr, and I just saw the talent that Coach had been putting together. I also saw the type of people they were."

He gravitated to that and wanted to be part of it. He learned early that it wouldn't be easy to be part of an up-and-coming program that eventually would become one of college basketball's powerhouses. In fact, Mason said in *Tales from the Arizona Wildcats Hardwood* that freshmen who went to Arizona often wanted to leave. It was the tough ones who stayed. "Especially kids from the big city," he said. "I came from L.A. Here I am in Tucson and I spent more time on the bench than I wanted to. It was hot. We ran a lot. Coach Olson was hard on us. But over the course of the year, by the end of my freshman year, I didn't want to leave. I stayed the summer, went to school, and worked out. So it was a pretty quick transition from being uncomfortable and being unhappy to being stimulated and challenged and excited. And that happened in the course of about eight months, maybe a year."

Bobbi Olson played a part in his and the other players' happiness. She'd often go to the back of the bus and ask how the players were doing in what Mason Jr. called a "counseling session" for the younger guys, maybe for all the guys. "She'd ask about our girlfriends, the parents, everything," he said. "Coach Olson wouldn't do that. We knew he cared about that, too, but he didn't get into those type of details a lot of the time. That's why they're such a good team. Mrs. Olson was the team mom and she was the one who connected with us on that level. But we knew in a weird way when we were talking to Mrs. Olson, we were probably talking to Coach as well. There was a little of that tightrope walk where you didn't want to say too much, but you also wanted to let her know what was going on in your life. She was very helpful. That was the kind of cool power dynamic the two of them had. And if Coach had anything that he wasn't as adept at, Mrs. Olson made up for it."

Mason Jr. remembers the exit meetings with Lute Olson and that they were helpful in his improvement as a player. "He would certainly talk to you about real specific things about your game,"

Harvey Mason Jr. (right) and son Trey Mason (left)
(Courtesy Harvey Mason Jr.)

he said. "He was very organized. He handed me a paper at the end of the meeting. He was optimistic. I wasn't feeling particularly optimistic, but he was...He said they were counting on big things from me. He gave me a list of things to work on. You can tell he spent some time on it and gave it some thought. It impressed me. He took the time to give me real, constructive feedback. If you're smart—and a lot of times I wasn't when I was 18 years old—you can take that and put it to good use. I thought that was cool."

The notes—like everything else Olson did—were meticulous. "He'd have every minute planned out on a piece of paper he'd either hold, keep in his pocket, or keep in his waistband," Mason Jr. said. "Every once in a while, he'd set it down on the table. In between doing drills, we'd all sneak over there and try to look at it and see what's coming up."

During those meticulously-planned meetings, he'd instruct, talk fundamentals, and motivate players. The latter he would tailor to each player. "It was different for different players," Mason Jr. said. "He absolutely got on me. He yelled at me but never cussed, never once. He'd point out all the things I was doing wrong. He knew that I needed to be challenged. That was the thing with Coach Olson. He figured out the personalities and who was going to react to what. And I didn't think I was gonna react to the way he was coaching, but I did because I learned a lot. My high school coach was a big yeller, and Coach Olson recognized that. He saw where I came from and so he was very critical of me. He did not hesitate to point out when I was making a mistake."

At one point, Mason hated it. That's why he wanted to leave. "You feel so mistreated and you feel like a piece of meat," he said. "But you don't have the right perspective when you're 18 to understand that. Some people probably do—like Steve Kerr or somebody who's a little bit more mature—but I was 18 coming out of high school. I scored 35 points a game in high school."

He then arrived at Arizona and was coached hard. "The criticism breaks you down, but that's part of Coach's program, which was to change your thinking," he said. "It was to set a tone and a culture for all the players of the program and to make sure they were all aligned and then rebuild people back up within the system, which is very smart, and I get it now, but at that point, I was reticent to accept it and hesitant to buy into it when I was 18 years old. Once we had broken the habit, then you can build it back up in the team concept. That's what he did."

Those methods were very frustrating for Mason Jr. at first. It took until his junior year for things to really click. "We went to the Final Four [my sophomore year] and [were] winning a lot, so the frustrations were a lot easier to swallow," he said. "I was on the bench playing for the No. 1 team in the country. I was playing a little bit, but we were all working for a common goal. The thing about playing for Coach Olson, it was about the bigger picture. It was about being a team and being a family. He instilled that in us."

Mason played behind some pretty good players: Lofton, Matt Muehlebach, and Kerr. "I wasn't too realistic with that because I thought I was better than everybody," he said, laughing. "To be that kind of player, you have to have that confidence and ego."

In a recent interview with ESPN, Mason Jr. was asked what he got from his college experience that translated into life and his approach. "It's really simple. When you're 18 you come in and you think you're at this level. You think you've really pushed yourself, you've maxed out. You've worked, you've practiced, you've done all this to get to this good place. So you come to the University of Arizona to get coached by Lute Olson," he said. "And you get there, you realize there's so much more potential, so much more room for growth and improvement than even I thought was possible. I thought I reached it. I thought I hit the ceiling of where I was gonna go, and Coach Olson rips that off... It takes a minute to understand that he's not doing it for himself, and there's no agenda other than to make you better and to make the team better. The thing that I took from Coach was the level of expectation above and beyond what I had for myself. It wasn't only Coach but the culture of the program. It was everybody."

Mason Jr. got better and later started alongside Muehlebach, helping Arizona to become the No. 1 team in the country in 1989. It was Elliott's senior year, and Jud Buechler, Muehlebach, and Lofton were all part of the team. Arizona fell to UNLV in the Sweet 16 on a last-second shot by Anderson Hunt.

Then, late in his senior year—with Arizona once again having a very good season—Mason Jr. suffered a torn ACL midway through the season. He came back for one game—on Senior Day, though he knew his career was over. He played three weeks after his surgery but with a knee brace. But he got hurt again later in the game. He actually had pulled off a dunk earlier in the game. "I had [one last] shining moment," he said, laughing.

Through his unbelievable world now, he has another "One Shining Moment." Given his music background, Mason Jr. produced the music for the updated theme for college basketball's NCAA Tournament, which uses the vocals of Jennifer Hudson. Since he graduated, Mason Jr. has become one of the world leaders in the music industry. He's a producer, songwriter, and CEO of the Record Academy.

Mason Jr. has carved out a great post-basketball career for himself and he attributes much of that success to Olson. "He affected me in every aspect of my life," Mason said. "It may have taken me some time to understand what he was doing to help us learn or what his system was, but what he wanted from us was to be successful young men. When it hit me, I realized his impact. It's a part of what I do now and my music career. I told him that many times. I told him he created a person who was competitive but a person who also tried to treat people the right way. I try to be respectful and be humble. What I learned also was the level of dedication to excellence. If you're going to do anything great, you have to work at it. He'd say he didn't care what we did, but it was about how you did it. If you're going to keep your locker, make it neat. If you're going to wear a uniform, wear it right. If you're going to shovel dirt, make sure you're going to get it all off the ground. He said, 'Don't do things halfway and [do things] in a way you'd be proud.' I've attempted to do that with all my businesses."

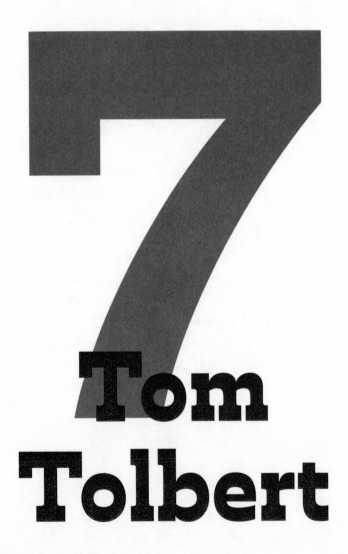

7

Tom Tolbert

No player gave more grief—intentional or otherwise—to Lute Olson than Tom Tolbert.

Sure, there were players that had to be dismissed or suspended a time or two during Olson's 25 years, but no player got under his skin more than Tolbert. Sometimes in a playful way. Sometimes in an irritating way. What's clear was they had a great admiration for one another during and after Tolbert's playing days in the mid-to-late 1980s. What's also clear: Tolbert's arrival at Arizona created one of the best nicknames for a coach in Arizona sports history: Midnight Lute.

It was the name then-UNLV coach Jerry Tarkanian coined for him after Tolbert had changed his mind, going from UNLV to Arizona. "I committed to UNLV early in the season," Tolbert said. "I like Vegas as a lot of people know. My parents used to visit Vegas. Occasionally, my friends would go to Vegas, and it was also close to [Lakewood, California,] where my parents could drive to all the games. And they played Irvine [the first school he attended], so I thought that was cool to play them again."

UNLV was the first school—of the big schools—to offer Tolbert a scholarship after he attended junior college. Clemson came in, too. He visited that ACC school in South Carolina. "I felt that was a different country after that plane flight," he said. "It was so far away."

Then came Arizona, where he visited and "had a good time" on his recruiting trip. "I was still gonna go to Vegas," he said. "I gave those guys my word. But I did love Arizona. I loved Lute and Bobbi was awesome. The [players] were great."

The allure of playing in the then-Pac-10 was nice. His parents would be able to see him when UA played UCLA and USC, and Arizona was close enough for them to visit for other games. "Again, I gave UNLV my word...but at the very last minute, I thought if I go to Vegas, it could end up being a mess," he said, laughing. "I loved the direction the Arizona program was going and decided to go there."

So, he changed his mind. On Signing Day then-UNLV assistant Mark Warkentien called to see if he was ready to sign to be a Runnin' Rebel. "They weren't happy," he said. "It wasn't a fun conversation to have. He wasn't pleased, but said I needed to speak to Tark because I owed it to him."

They set up a 5:00 PM call so he'd be able to speak to Tarkanian. Later the day, Tolbert realized he had to go see his younger brother play in a Little League game. He figured he could be late to the game. He waited 10 minutes, then 20 minutes for Tark. "I figured they said, 'Screw it.' So I left for the game," he said. "I went to the game. I come back later, and my neighbor asked if we were expecting somebody. I said no. They say, 'Well, somebody pulled up in a black town car, got out of the back seat, an older bald guy. He knocked, then went to the window, and knocked again. He then got in the car and left.'"

The neighbor had obviously just described Tarkanian. "I guess it was a good thing I wasn't there," he said.

Midnight Lute was born. A couple of years later, Olson went in Vegas and got Matt Othick to play at Arizona to reinforce the nickname. "There was nothing underhanded going on," Tolbert said. "I had second thoughts on what it would be like for me in the city of Las Vegas as opposed to being in the city of Tucson."

As it turned out, UNLV went to the Final Four in what would have been Tolbert's junior year, and Arizona went to the Final Four for the first time school history in 1988. When Tolbert arrived in Tucson, he loved the city, the campus, the program, and Olson. "Obviously, Lute is so impressive in the way he carries himself, and I won't be breaking any news, but all the moms loved him," he said. "He exuded head coach, and parents loved that. They felt that if their son was going there, they'd be looked after. He had a professionalism about him and a sense of class that you couldn't help but be impressed. And you know he's a no-nonsense guy, but he also had a better sense of humor than most people know. I'm sure it wasn't the same recruiting visit that [former Arizona State head coach] Bill Frieder would give, I'd imagine. But there was nothing that was not impressive about Lute. His resume coming from Iowa spoke for itself. And how people spoke about of him—who he was and how he carried himself."

Once the players were part of the program, Olson would often have them get in shape by running around the campus mall where there is about a mile-long area. Tolbert was notorious for being, well, different. "I didn't think about Lute when I was hiding in the back. I was just tired of running around the mall," he said. "We had to run around it twice."

To make sure the players actually ran the course, UA coaches sent managers or grad assistants to check in on their progress. Tolbert, along with the others, ran around and took the first lap. The route is mostly visible from everywhere, save for a blind spot or two, and, of course, Tolbert noticed that. "I always noticed a fountain there and I think, *Hell, I'm going to jump in the fountain. I'm not running this. I'm tired. And I'm tired of practice anyway.* So, I just jumped in the fountain and laid there in the fountain.

From left to right: Lute Olson, Bruce Fraser, Matt Muehlebach, and Tom Tolbert (Courtesy Matt Muehlebach)

I put my whole body in there except for my head. No one could really see me. Sooner or later, our manager, Nick, comes over and looks around to look for people. He just happens to look into the fountain, makes a double-take, and sees me. I just put my finger to my lips to let him know to be quiet about it. He just started laughing and he just kept walking, but I told him to let me know when the last guys were coming through so I can go. I didn't want the coaches to think anything was out of the ordinary because I was always at the back of the pack anyway. Eventually, I got out, and because it was a time when the weather was still warm, my clothes were able to dry enough to make it look like I was really sweating and working hard."

Once he was done, he heard someone say, "Way to work, Tom." "I walked by with a little laughter," he said. "I don't know if I told anybody, but it was only Nick and I that knew that I took a little dip."

Olson eventually found out…years later. "I told him, and he said he knew, but I'm not sure he did," Tolbert said. "I was kind of embarrassed to tell him because, hey, he was still Lute. I didn't want to disappoint him. He gave me that look and rolled his eyes."

Eye rolls happened constantly, particularly at practices—and perhaps games—because Olson constantly got on Tolbert and his desire not to play defense, often teasing that the court leaned to one side because Tolbert was waiting on one end to play offense. Olson got on Tolbert for a reason. He wanted him to be better. "Ultimately, he saw someone that had more than he was giving," Tolbert said. "It took me a while to kind of figure it out. I don't know if there was ever a moment when I didn't think

I was working as hard as I could. I was doing everything he was asking. He always wanted more and was always getting on me about something. In my career I was able to pretty much handle them getting on me or yelling at me. I'm sure I deserved to get yelled at because I wasn't working as hard as I could have. He was the one that wouldn't let it go and just kept on me and kept on me then kept on me some more."

Olson often told the story that after practice one day, he went home and said something was different about practice. He couldn't put his finger on it...until he did. "He told Bobbi, 'I didn't have to get on Tom today,'" Tolbert said. "It was the first day I didn't have to get on Tom about something. I always enjoyed that story because apparently his badgering of me throughout a year and a half or more meant that I finally got it. I mean, it wasn't easy at times. I often thought, *Why is it always me that he gets on? Always me, not Sean [Elliott], not Steve [Kerr], not Anthony [Cook], not anyone?* But I took it and wore it and tried to get better. So, I tried hard."

He felt at times he was being picked on. But he realized later that Olson got on him because he needed Tolbert to help get the team where it needed to get to. "I'm sure he felt it was his responsibility as a coach to get me to that point," he said. "Ultimately, he did. I'm sure it wasn't all that fun for him either. I'm sure he wanted me to learn a lot quicker."

When talking to his kids or up-and-coming players, Tolbert now uses that experience under Olson as a teaching tool. And he appreciated the tough love more once he wasn't getting it. "I say, 'When you are tired, you probably have more than you think you do.' Lute saw that in me, that I had more to give than what I was giving," he said. "You can get back on defense, you can communicate on defense better, you can do whatever was needed to be done. Sometimes players can't see that, and it took me a while to see it. It's not the most fun ride to go through, but at the end of it, you're happy. I'm glad he did because if he didn't, who knows if I ever make it to the NBA? I never would have figured out that I had to do a lot of the little things in the NBA if I didn't have him."

He said he never regrets his decision to change his mind from UNLV to Arizona. "I never would have met Steve Kerr," he said. "I would have never gone to the Final Four with guys like Craig McMillan. My best friend is Craig Bergman, who I golf with frequently. I had great teammates in Sean Elliott and Anthony Cook, who I still keep in touch with. [I] still talk to Jud Buechler. They were a great group of guys. I met my wife, Laurie. I played in a great town for college basketball and just a great college town, and the fans were awesome."

As for ever mentioning the name Midnight Lute to Lute, well, that never happened. "I did get a kick out of Bob Baffert having a horse named Midnight Lute," he said. "And it was a big-time horse."

Named for a big-time coach.

8

Jud Buechler

Jud Buechler wanted to be a college volleyball player and then, well, maybe a professional volleyball player. It's likely he made the right choice in picking basketball, though he always had a passion for volleyball as an All-American high school volleyball player out of Poway High in California. It was Arizona and Lute Olson who swayed his decision to play basketball and to stick with it. "I was looking at schools that had both sports," Buechler said.

He had already visited a few schools—UCLA, Pepperdine, UC Santa Barbara—and then there was Arizona. "Arizona came in late into the recruitment," Buechler said. "They used to call him 'Midnight Lute,' but I'm not sure that applies to me."

Buechler said he'll never forget the time Olson went for his in-home visit with the Buechlers and the impact he had. "He walked into the house, and immediately I felt a connection with him," he said. "I was about 17 years old and I just felt safe with him. It was at a time when you're leaving your home for the very first time, leaving your parents, and he made me feel safe. I felt like this man was going to look after me. I don't know if that's a father figure. I guess it falls into that category."

Olson had that presence, that aura. "Coach just had a way about him," he said. "He came in and just wowed the family with his charm, his humor, and his intelligence."

Of course, Buechler's mom was impressed. Most every mom of every recruit was impressed. "Absolutely," he said. "He was Hollywood-good looking, charismatic. But it was everything he brought to the table. How could moms not?"

And if moms were swayed, how could they not have a say in where their sons went? "But to be sure it wasn't about that," Buechler said. "He was authentic. His talks weren't cheesy or a schmoozing. That's not what it was. It was just his character and his charisma."

Not long after, Buechler was committed to Arizona and signed.

It was the mid-1980s, and Arizona was becoming one of the best programs in the country. Sean Elliott was there. Steve Kerr was there. Kenny Lofton, Tom Tolbert, Craig McMillan were all at Arizona. The Wildcats were on the verge of their first Final Four and so much more. And Olson was the architect of it all. "He was old school. I wouldn't consider him a players' coach, at least when I was there at Arizona," Buechler said. "At Arizona there was this separation where he was the coach, and we were the players. It was the assistants who looked after us. He was the head honcho. Once our careers were over, we got closer. He'd get closer to players then. But there were no real surprises when I got there. We had great assistants back then: Ricky Birdsong, Kevin O'Neill, Tony McAndrews, and Scott Thompson. They bridged the gap. They were looking out for us and kept us connected every day and made sure everything was all right. Coach was the CEO with the big office. I think I only went in his office but twice in four years and I was a senior then. He looked over everything and I was okay with that. He had such a presence when he showed up and when he did you got your act together. You stood upright."

He didn't remember much about the two meetings, though one was to talk about the team and the other was so that he

From left to right: Lute Olson, Bruce Fraser, and Jud Buechler (Courtesy Matt Othick)

could become roommates with Brian Williams. (He did, and the good friends became teammates not only in college, but also in the NBA with the Chicago Bulls and Detroit Pistons.) But those office meetings could be a less-than-desirable situation. "I remember getting called into his office was like getting called into the principal's office," he said. "You weren't really comfortable before you went in. But then you go in and—being the captain—you realize everything is going to be okay."

Everything was more than okay. In fact, Buechler's four years were some of the best in Arizona history. There were great wins and a lot of them. Arizona went 107–26. It was—and still is—the greatest four-year stretch in Arizona basketball history. Along the way, Arizona played in its first Final Four, two Sweet 16s, and an NCAA Tournament second-round game. There were some great highs and some crushing lows. "My four years were more than I could ask for in a college experience," he said. "There was so much there for growth and being a human being. What Coach Olson did that was great was he brought in incredible players. It was important to him that he bring in guys/players who had high character. Of course, over time there were some wild ones, but in my time, there were the Steve Kerrs, the Bruce Frasers, the Harvey Masons. These guys are still my best friends. It was an incredibly special four years for me. When we see each other at events or reunions, it's really a special thing because we all meant so much to each other during those years."

The only two big-time recruits at the time were McMillan and Elliott. "He had a knack of finding those diamonds in the rough," Buechler said. "He'd say, 'Let's get these guys and develop them.' It allowed him to go after the five-stars later in his career."

While going through it all, Buechler said he didn't think much about what Olson was doing, just that he was doing it. While others came in as some of the best players on their teams and areas and decided to transfer, Buechler never thought about that. The competition was fierce, but Buechler was a grinder. "I was at the first practice and I had to play one-on-one with Rolf Jacobs and Sean Elliott," he said. "It lasted for 15 minutes, and I don't think I scored a basket. Sean and Rolf were very good. But that was the reality of it, and reality hits you in the face, and you have to step up. I wasn't in high school anymore. I'm not on my club team. This was the best of the best here, and we're all battling for playing time. I'd go back to my dorm room and ask, 'Can I play here? Am I going to play? Can I do this?' There's some doubt. But I don't think I ever questioned [transferring]. I never wanted to leave."

Buechler said every player must have gone through that kind of self-doubt, but he knew he'd get better under Olson. "He was such an incredible teacher of the game," he said. "He taught the fundamentals of the game and appreciated the fundamentals. And I always just felt, *I'm just gonna keep playing as hard as I can and see what happens, see where this goes, and keep trying to get better.* I know a lot of guys wanted to leave. Some left; some came back. It was about playing time and stuff. For me, I wasn't going anywhere. I was gonna ride it out whether I played or I didn't play. I was fortunate enough to play so it worked out fine."

As for the highs and lows, the players went through them. So did Olson, and he handled them in his way, specifically the loss to Oklahoma in 1988 in the semifinals of the Final Four and a last-second loss to UNLV in the Sweet 16 a year later. "What I do know is that he was incredibly proud of our accomplishments," Buechler said. "Obviously, there was disappointment we felt that year, but it was a magical run [in 1988]. I remember me thinking, *Okay, we didn't do it, but we're knocking on the door.* I think that year was the year we turned Tucson into a basketball town. It may have been more of a football town then. But that's when we got on the map."

In 1989 Arizona, the No. 1 team in the country, lost to UNLV when Anderson Hunt hit the game-winner over Lofton. It seemed devasting. "That was a tough one," Buechler said. "It's tricky when you're No. 1 because you're expected to win it. But you need a little luck. Looking back, it was a bummer. But what a great two-year stretch. It's hard to say how he felt. We were disappointed. I don't remember him and his emotions. I do remember him thinking we're going to continue to work hard and get better, and that at some point, we'd break through. He was proud of us."

He continued being proud—as was the case for many of his ex-players—when they were in the NBA. He'd often show up for games. By then the relationship had gone from coach to friend. Olson attended contests during the Bulls' run to an NBA title in 1997 when they had Kerr, Williams, and Buechler on the team. He showed up at weddings or big events. "It was fun being an adult around him," Buechler said, laughing. "It was better than when you're a player because of what comes with that…It was amazing because everything shifted. He would reach out occasionally. What I really loved as we moved on with our careers and I'd watch Arizona play, I didn't know many of the guys. But I knew Lute. He was the common denominator. You'd be able to turn on the TV and watch, and he was the one who connected the team to me."

And, of course, he misses him. "Absolutely," he said. "He is Arizona basketball. I still feel very passionate about Arizona basketball because of him. He was the one that really made it that way for all of us."

He'll always be thankful for him. Buechler credits him for instilling the belief that every day was an opportunity to get better as a human being or a basketball player. Olson was almost like a father figure. "Besides my dad, he's the next most influential person in my life," he said. "Those years when you're so impressionable and you're trying to figure out who you are, you're under his watch. He taught me hard work, competitiveness, and that never-giving-up attitude—all those things that come along when you're playing for a great coach. There was integrity, too. Without him my life would be completely different. I know in my heart that my life wouldn't be the same. It wouldn't be as good."

9

Channing Frye

Arizona center Channing Frye may have a couple of former Arizona State players to thank for getting noticed. And given the end result, that's okay. Former UA coach Jay John had been looking at a couple of players in Phoenix, where there happened to be this lanky kid named Channing Frye. He played at St. Mary's High School. He was a blip on the radar as a sophomore when Arizona started noticing him. "He was like, 'Who is this kid?'" Frye said, remembering what John had said.

Then Lute Olson went to a few practices and then a bunch of games. By his junior year, Frye was starting to get noticed even more. Later in the recruiting process, he met Lute and Bobbi Olson, and one of the first things they said was: "Goodness gracious, you look like Sean Elliott."

The Elliott comparisons still occur for Frye. "Especially when I go down to Tucson," he said.

When he was being recruited, he was able to meet Jason Gardner, Gilbert Arenas, and Luke Walton. He already knew Richard Jefferson since he's from Phoenix, too. "I committed the end of my junior year," Frye said. "That was a big deal because I started to become who I was going to be in college."

About that time he was starting to get letters from other blue-blood schools like North Carolina and Kansas. "I said, 'No, I'd rather go to UA,'" he said. "It was the way Coach Olson talked to me. It felt like a family. The fact that they didn't just guarantee me something. They would say, 'You're gonna have to work and you're gonna be part of a really good recruiting class.' I thought that was pretty awesome."

Olson was so good at evaluating talent and had the ability to coach them up if he found that they lacked something. And for a player like Frye, who was a top 100 player (98th overall, according to Hoop Scoop), Olson knew he could make him better. "It was crazy," Frye said. "I think Coach O gave players a pretty blank canvas. He just said, 'Stay within the lines.' The biggest thing was just don't worry about the end result. Just focus on the process. Coach Olson was structured. I'd go to ASU and watch them practice [when I was being recruited]. I was like this is a hot bunch of mess. I'm not trying to be disrespectful, just honest."

He saw why ASU was losing and why the program wasn't consistent. "I'd come down to UA, and everything was down to the minute," Frye said. "I'm watching Gilbert Arenas, Michael Wright, Loren Woods, Richard Jefferson, Luke Walton, Jason Gardner, Ricky Anderson, and whoever else was there. The dudes where flying around the court like it's a game."

During one of the visits, Channing's father, Tom, turned to him while watching them play and said, "You can get so much better and quicker here."

By the time Frye graduated high school, he was ready to get to Arizona to get ready for the season. Two days after graduation, he was rooming with Dennis Latimore. By then Frye said

Coach John told him he might have to be redshirted because the roster was so loaded. "I probably said something a little nicer than this, but I was like, 'Man, fuck you. I'm not redshirting,'" he recalled. "It was just my attitude, and I think they liked that. I think sometimes they put up with me because they knew I had an attitude. I was like, 'Hell, no you're not going to dictate my future like that.'"

So, he got in the weight room and bulked up from 210 to 235. He spent the summers in Tucson trying to get better. He learned from Gardner and Walton. He took in everything. And he listened to Olson. "You know Coach was really saying more like, 'You just got to play.' He just talked to me. That was the thing about Coach," Frye said. "This is how cool Coach was. During my junior year, I thought it would be okay to take a lot of classes where I could graduate and do this and that. So, for a month I was waking up early at 6:00 AM, then going to class, and then going to another class at 6:00 at night."

It was a busy schedule, to be sure. Frye knew it. Everyone knew it. "Coach ends up pulling me into his office and saying, 'I know school is important. And this is a huge year for you. How can we make this work? How can we talk to somebody to help you figure this out?' I loved that he was out there looking out for me. He knew I was tired, and a lot of it was school stuff," Frye said. "Then he said he was getting a lot of calls about me [from NBA types] so let's not lose track of what's important for you right now because you've worked so hard. He was like a father figure at times to me. He then said he wanted more leadership from me, that I needed to be more vocal, and that 'Not everyone has to like you all the time.' That really resonated with me."

There was another incident involving a class when he wanted to change his major and got pushback from the professor. Olson went with him to talk to the teacher. "And he didn't have to do that," Frye said. "He didn't have to stick up for me and he saw me getting upset and he was just like to the professor, 'Do you even know what this guy does for the community? This young man is trying to make sure that he's prepared after he leaves the UA.' I was like, 'Damn, Coach,' and it made me just want to go play harder for him."

There was no better example of Olson defending Frye than when Frye had an unbelievable stretch at Washington and Washington State. Frye went 24-for-28 from the floor and 8-for-8 from the free throw line. Olson sent a letter to the Pac-10 office,

Channing Frye (AP Images)

scolding conference officials for not naming Frye the Player of the Week. "It was a seething letter and it was great," Frye said. "But again, as tough as he was on us at practice, this man would go to war for you when he felt you deserved it. I wasn't going to advocate for myself, but he did. Again, he was like a father figure. I was just putting my head down and trying to win games. And he was like, 'Give this kid some credit.'"

Like many of his players, Frye referred to Olson as a "father figure." Of course, Olson was also a figure who had to deal with Frye's parents. "First of all, he deserves a medal for dealing with my parents," Frye said, laughing. "But he was an extension of them. When I got my first tattoo, he was like, 'What are you doing?' And when I got home, my parents were like, 'What are you doing?' For me it was like his word was just like my parents' words. He'd get on me before they would."

Olson emphasized to not waste any opportunity he had been given. Frye took the words to heart and still does more than 16 years later. "Coach knew how to make men," he said. "You don't make men by telling them what to do, by telling them to go here or go there, to do this and to do that. *Don't go have fun, stay in the gym.* He didn't tell people that. He just said, 'Hey, listen, this is what I expect. You can't just walk on the court and expect to be good. You have to put the time in.'"

Sage advice. In addition to calling Olson a father figure, Frye also compared him and his assistants to other branches of the family tree. "We didn't want to let him down or any of our coaching staff down, but for me it was like playing for my grandpa, and the coaching staff were like uncles," Frye said. "We could talk to coach Rodney Tension, coach Jim Rosborough, coach Josh Pastner about anything for the most part. If we went out on a Saturday night, they knew we'd be there on Sunday, so they trusted us, and that trust you didn't want to break. Nothing was more important than us doing our job. That is why all of Coach Olson's players do so well in the NBA because they had this thing: don't make excuses, do your job. What is your job? Do that, and then everyone else can trust you. You had so much pride in making sure you did your job."

Olson instilled a lot of values in him, including the importance of preparation. "I learned that there's a right way to play basketball," Frye said. "But to feel good about it, you got to do the work beforehand. That's the weight room, there's the mental part, there's the teamwork. All that goes into a game. Preparation was key. Heck, I was prepared for a damn hurricane because Coach prepared us for it. He was upfront with everything. That's how I am today. I try to be as prepared as possible. He'd tell you the good things and the bad things. But again, the biggest thing was to just do your job. Do what's required of you. If it means to open a door for a lady, you do that."

Before the 2012 season, Frye was diagnosed with an enlarged heart that kept him from playing that year. Olson was one of the first people to call him. Later in Frye's career, they traveled together to Hawaii to do a clinic. "I had a great relationship with him," Frye said. "He'd keep up with all of us. I wasn't the best at reaching out to everyone all the time, but whenever I was in Phoenix if we played, most of the time he was there. When we won the championship in Cleveland, he texted me. Those things were pretty big."

So, of course, Frye misses his coach, the one who helped him with a great college career and who set him up for success in the NBA. "I do miss him," he said. "I wish I would have gone back more to see him and just visit with him. I was kind of dealing with my own things with my parents [who passed]. And I was trying to get my own life going. I think I could have leaned on him a little bit more than I did with myself. But I do miss him."

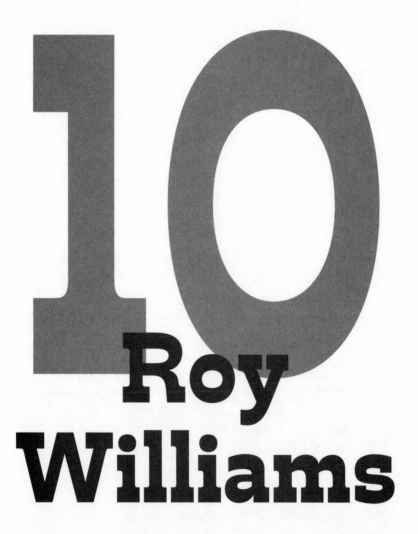

10
Roy
Williams

It was the spring of 1980, and a young assistant coach named Roy Williams met an older coach in Lute Olson. Williams was 30 years old, and the 46-year-old Olson had just led Iowa to the Final Four before losing to Louisville in the semifinals. They happened to be on the same flight after an event. "Lute and Bobbi were on the flight, so I stopped to talk to him as I was going to my seat," Williams said. "They had a great run. I spoke to them for a couple of minutes."

At the time, Williams was an assistant coach at the University of North Carolina under Dean Smith. Later that summer, the two ran into one another again on the recruiting circuit, sitting beside one another, and struck up a friendship. Coach to coach. Eventually friend to friend. "For a few years we'd be on the road, and I'd see him," Williams said. "I started calling him 'Granddaddy.' He just laughed at me, telling me that I'm not too young myself. We had a good time."

It's a friendship that lasted until Olson's passing in 2020. It also was a friendship that saw the two coaching titans meet in huge games and in huge moments throughout the 1990s and 2000s. "I admired his coaching and his mannerisms, his personality, his ethics, his moral standing," Williams said. "I liked everything about him and I loved the fact he was such a nice person but very competitive. I loved those things."

Williams said it was a respectful relationship from his end. "But apparently he liked my company," Williams joked.

He recalled one summer the two worked at the annual Michael Jordan Fantasy Camp, where many of the high-profile college coaches assisted at the camp, coaching teams of adult men. They worked together coaching a team as co-coaches. Another time they were together on a Nike coaching trip in Hawaii where there were dinners and functions scheduled. "They had this big dinner set up, and I turned to Lute and said, 'What would you think about this?' There are [coaches] going on this big thing, and they're going to do all these crazy games, and I don't drink at all, and Lute never really drank very much," Williams said. "I told him, 'Why don't you and Bobbi, me, and Wanda not go? I've got reservations out here looking over the ocean. It would be just for us.' He said, 'God Almighty, Bobbi would kiss you'...So we went on this wonderful dinner that night."

That's the type of relationship they had as fast, comfortable friends. "We would call each other periodically," he said. "We just enjoyed each other's company. As we got older, we played golf together on a couple of coach's trips. He was a guy I admired."

Perhaps because his one-time boss—Smith—had similar qualities. "They did," he said. "Coach Smith believed in doing things the right way. He cared about the kids. It wasn't just about winning games. It was about giving them a chance to be able to be more productive in society and not just think about a basketball bouncing, and I felt like that's the way Lute coached also.

He wanted to win. He was fiercely competitive but also what was important was how those kids did after basketball."

It wasn't until 1988—the year Arizona defeated Smith and Williams—that Williams became the head coach at Kansas. "That's when we became even closer," he said.

Even when they competed against one another, they'd often speak to each other before they played. "We were friends, and it

Roy Williams (AP Images)

didn't make any difference about what happened in the game," he said. "I trusted him, he trusted me, and we believed in the same things. We believe in things ethically and morally, coaching the heck out of your kids."

Featuring future NBA pros like Paul Pierce, Scot Pollard, Raef LaFrentz, and Jacque Vaughn, Kansas was the best team in the country in 1997, and Arizona upset the No. 1-seeded Jayhawks in the Sweet 16. "[It was] one of my lowest points of my entire career," Williams said. "It really was because I thought our team was really good."

Williams recalled Arizona having a good team, too, that had suffered some injuries or problems during the season. And, indeed, it did with Miles Simon out half the season with academic issues. Arizona eventually finished fifth in the Pac-10, getting into the NCAA Tournament as a No. 4 seed. "Then all of a sudden, they got it together with that great backcourt of Mike Bibby, Mike Dickerson, Jason Terry," Williams said. "Jerod Haase was limited with a broken wrist and couldn't shoot the ball. He played 12 minutes and made just one basket. Arizona made a great run. We had a chance at the end to tie it but didn't. Arizona was great. It was the year they beat three No. 1 seeds to win it."

No team has done it since.

Just a year earlier, Arizona faced Kansas in Denver at the Sweet 16. Arizona had Kansas on the ropes in the final minutes of the game, but Haase was able to hit a big shot from the corner in the game's final seconds to advance. Arizona then played Kansas twice in 2002–03. As the No. 1 team in the nation visiting Allen Fieldhouse, Arizona won big behind Salim Stoudamire. Later that year—in a huge Elite Eight game in Anaheim, California—Kansas won 78–75 to advance to the Final Four.

Whenever Williams faced Olson, it required total preparation. "That's the best way to describe it because for us they were not going to make mistakes and help us. So, we had to be at the top of our game," he said. "We beat Duke a game before [in the Sweet 16], then turned around and played Arizona. Those two games were pretty sizable tests for us. They had Luke Walton, Jason Gardner. Arizona's kids were great. We went after each other as hard as we could. It was total respect from the players and the coaches. It was big-time college basketball at its greatest level."

Williams' team advanced to the national championship game before losing to Syracuse. He then left Kansas after that season to become the head coach at North Carolina. The two faced each other two more times. Before Arizona faced the Tar Heels in 2006, Williams invited Olson and a couple of his traveling party over for a quick get-together at his home before Arizona was scheduled to go get dinner. Olson and the others went for a quick visit. "They came by, and I asked Lute if he wanted something to drink, and he said, 'Sure, but what do you have?' I said, 'Coke, Diet Sprite, and I have some wine,'" Williams said. "It's so funny because I don't drink. He said he'd have wine, but I wasn't sure how good it was because I don't drink it. People just give it to me. He looked at it and said, 'You have some good stuff here.'"

Williams offered up the wine, but there was a catch. Olson would have to open it because Williams didn't know how. "He started laughing, saying I was unbelievable," Williams said, laughing as he retold the story. "He came to our house to drink my wine and had to open it."

Arizona fell to the Tar Heels 86–69 the next day. A season later, North Carolina visited McKale Center in what was then one of the most anticipated games in Olson's final season, though no one knew he would retire. "We had Marcus Ginyard and Brandan Wright and we were pretty good," Williams said. "Brandan got sick; he had eaten something the night before. He was there laying on the floor in the locker room. What that did was brought us even more together; we were mentally as high as we could possibly be because we had a couple of guys coming off the bench who were all of a sudden starting. We were really good that day. We quieted the crowd. They were hardly into it because we were up something like 15 or 20. That was one of the best games we played all year."

Months later, Olson took a year off and then retired after the 2008 season.

No question he was respected in the college basketball world among his peers in the coaching fraternity. "They felt the same way I did," Williams said. "They thought he was a true gentleman, a guy you'd like your son to play for. Again, I had called him 'Granddaddy' all the time because he had taken me under his wings. Lute had that reputation as a good, solid person… who was fiercely competitive. And that's a pretty doggone good description of a coach."

Williams said Olson's competitiveness came out in the two Fantasy Camps they'd coached in. "We really enjoyed it, and it was fun, but during the course of the games, we'd get ticked off at our players, and they were 35-year-old guys," he said, laughing. "We'd snap at them. It was really funny. We thought if we're going to play a game, you might as well play the best you can."

It's indicative of the competitive-but-friendly type of relationship the two Hall of Fame basketball coaches had through the years. "He treated me like one of the guys," he said. "The first reaction when we'd see one another was he'd smile. And that made me feel good. Also, he cared about his players, and they cared about him. I told him one time, 'I would love for my son to play for you;' that's the biggest compliment you can give a coach. There were several of them, but there are several I wouldn't want that to happen."

Williams cherished his friendship with Olson and had great respect for him. "He was one of our game's giants," he said.

11
Matt Brase

There have been hundreds and hundreds of players Lute Olson coached through his five decades, but no one knew him better than Matt Brase. He came into this world on June 15, 1982, becoming one of Olson's many beloved grandchildren. Brase was an insider into the Olson family on so many levels during those many cherished years he was with "Poppa Lute."

It didn't take long to realize Poppa Lute, his famous and respected white-haired grandfather, was someone special. "We moved to Tucson when I was two years old, and I always saw him at work," Brase said. "And basketball was part of our family. We'd always have our family dinners at Poppa Lute's and Ma Bobbi's house every Sunday. I was there all the time. I was a ball boy for the games. That's all I knew."

He was this young kid hanging with the likes of Steve Kerr, Sean Elliott, and Tom Tolbert. He was all of six years old. "They were my best friends," he said.

He knew they were all special, including his grandfather, when he was young. But he really didn't know Olson's stature until he got older. "I always saw him in that leadership role, a mentor," Brase said. "He was the head of the family."

The impact of his grandfather's role didn't hit until he'd travel to Los Angeles with the family for away games. The atmosphere at those venues—UCLA's Pauley Pavilion and USC's Sports Arena—didn't have the same feel or fanbase McKale Center did. And many times UA fans rivaled opponent's crowds in numbers or noise. "I thought that was just college basketball," he said. "Then you start playing for him and going to other venues and you're wondering where everyone is at. No one is at those games like at Oregon State and Washington State. It's then I realized how special he made McKale and Tucson. No question Arizona was special compared to other spots."

Brase never once thought about playing for his grandfather, even though he was a high school player in Tucson and at Central Arizona College. In truth, he thought he wasn't good enough. It wasn't until players like Hassan Adams and Channing Frye—just to name a couple—convinced him to join the team as a walk-on. Former UA player John Ash, another walk-on, said he'd have the time of his life.

So, Brase made a call to Olson. "I called him to ask," Brase said. "And he was like, 'I just want you to know that you're going to be a practice player, and there will be little game time.'"

Olson then talked to associate head coach Jim Rosborough and the rest of the coaching staff. "He thought it was a great idea, but he didn't want my expectations to be too high," Brase said. "I was like, 'Let's do this.'"

He was inside more than ever. He was not only Coach's grandson, but also his player. Did he find out anything about his grandfather that he didn't already know? "Not really because I grew up at McKale," he said. "It was more so when I was on the coaching staff that I found out. He was so detailed with practice plans. Practices were to the minute in his plans, and he'd hand-write everything. He talked about it all. He was so precise. That's when I really got to see the behind the scenes…He let guys play in practice. He wouldn't stop the practice to make a point. It could be a couple of plays to let them get through it and then stop it and make his point. He never slowed the practices. In fact, that helped me with my practices."

From practices to games, everything was on point with him. His players knew what exactly to expect in games because they had gone over everything in practice. As for being a player, it was special for Brase, though he rarely played. Ash was right: he had

Matt Brase (Courtesy Jody Brase)

the time of his life. But did his teammates ever think he was a spy for Olson? "Heck, I had already been around the program for a long time. So everyone trusted me," Brase said, laughing. "They knew I wouldn't do that. But there were times when they'd say, 'Why is your grandpa so tough on me?'…But they trusted me. They knew nothing would get back to him."

The bond only grew when Brase became part of Olson's coaching staff in an administrative role for the basketball operations department. "I loved it, being that close and being in staff meetings," he said. "I was able to learn more about the basketball side of it, his teaching methods. Our relationship didn't change but maybe made it that much stronger because we spent more time together."

One thing that was very apparent was where the team would eat. It had to be good. "He was big on his restaurants on the road," Brase said. "We'd eat at great places, steakhouses [and such] and we'd be in and out in 45 minutes. He made sure we were in and out, very efficient."

No time was tougher for the Olsons than when Lute's beloved wife of more than 40 years became deathly ill in late 2000 while Arizona had one of the best teams in school history. Lute never let on his wife had been extremely ill despite going to the hospital every day—and night—before and after practice. He eventually missed the championship game of the Fiesta Bowl Classic. It was an indication things were not good with Bobbi.

A few days later—on New Year's Eve of 2001—she passed away. "I remember having so many people around and everyone being so gracious, bringing in food, catering in food. It seemed to go on for days. Everyone loved him. They wanted to make sure he was going to be okay," Brase said. "There were two games in there [when Olson was still on a leave of absence], and we went back in his room and watched the games together, just me and him…everyone else would still be hanging out, and we went back over and we just watched the game. You could just see it was a good outlet for him to just be talking about the game. He'd be like: 'Why is this guy doing this or that'…but it helped him keep his mind off [things]."

Two weeks after Bobbi's death, Olson went back to work. "My mother just told him she's not coming back and that he should get back, that he had a job and obligation, and that sports are a beautiful thing," Brase said. "It might not solve a lot of problems, but it would take your mind off things."

Arizona went 18–3 the rest of the way, losing to Duke in the NCAA Championship Game.

But Brase saw so many of those good times off the court. Here was this iconic figure who loved to boogie board on the beach. He loved the golf course—and so much more. What he really enjoyed was coaching his guys. It was said a time or two that if all he did was coach his guys, he'd be okay with it. "He loved that," Brase said. "He loved the molding of the young men and he had so many success stories of people that didn't go on to play basketball for a living. He fostered such a great environment for these guys. He held them accountable. They'd take etiquette classes. People would ask, 'Why are we doing this?' But as you look back, you know why. It's very important."

Every moment between Brase and Olson mattered—whether it was on vacation at the family's summer home near San Diego or just at a wholesale store. "We spent so much time at Coronado

Island together," Brase said. "He'd be in Los Angeles a lot recruiting so then he'd come down after watching games. I was very fortunate to spend that much time with him…He loved going to Costco. He was very simple. We look at it—now that I can take a step back—and he was this famous guy and he didn't care. He was just this very simple guy from the Midwest. He wasn't flashy. Heck, he wore khakis with a blue blazer, maybe sometimes he'd wear a suit. I think that helped him be relatable with people in Tucson. He was strong and had that hair, that smile. It was just like he was like the perfect icon for Tucson. Look at it this way: he's not like an L.A. flashy guy."

It was one of the many reasons why Tucson—and Wildcats fans—loved him. Of course, there were the victories. But he was also visible in the community. "He had a busy schedule," Brase said. "But he knew that was part of his job. I couldn't tell you how many speaking engagements he had. I saw it firsthand for a couple of years being on the staff. But he didn't mind doing it. I think he just felt it was an honor to coach at Arizona. I never saw him put himself above anything else. There were charity and speaking engagements in town and on the road. He wanted everything to be inclusive. He always was trying to prove the program was a good one and be a better one. He wanted to make sure the players were involved, too. Some programs don't even do this anymore. He never said no to anything. They'd call the secretary, and she'd set it up. Any normal person's eyes would glaze over from everything he did."

Another unique thing was he always wrote letters and thank you cards when appropriate. "I remember as a kid when we were on planes, he'd pull out his little briefcase or whatever it was and just start writing thank you notes to anyone. He did that a lot," Brase said. "I'm not very good at writing letters, and that's the thing I wish I was better at. I remember doing something with the San Antonio Spurs while I was with Grand Canyon University and I remember Coach [Budenholzer] wrote me back after attending the event."

He received the letter within a week of the event. It said: "I learned from your grandfather that once you get a note from someone you handwrite one right back to [the person] and put it back in the mail."

Lesson learned for Brase, who was a Houston Rockets assistant from 2018 to 2020. He's now a coach with the Portland Trail Blazers.

Brase misses his grandfather, who taught him lessons in life and on the court, dearly. "So much," he said. "It's one of those things where there's not a day I don't think about him. [I] constantly think about just how you wish you could just call him or text him. I'm very, very fortunate that my family moved to Tucson when I was young. They lived just 10 minutes from the house and they were able to experience everything that I did. He was such a big part of our lives. To be able to play for him was great but not just because he was a Hall of Fame coach but because he was your grandpa and an incredible human. I don't have a lot of hobbies except for basketball and now I'm doing this—coaching some of the world's best players [in the NBA]. He set that foundation. Early in my life, I found my foundation and I just want to make him proud every day."

12
Josh Pastner

To say Josh Pastner is a favorite son of the Arizona basketball program would be an understatement. And that's after scoring just 38 points in 42 games. Still, Arizona fans love him.

The former walk-on-turned-assistant-coach-turned-Memphis-head-coach-turned-Georgia-Tech-head-coach can always return to Tucson and feel like he's never really left.

It all started with a letter—or letters—to Lute. And, well, any coach who would respond to his request of wanting to be part of the program. "Heck, I sent one to every school in America," Pastner said. "Coach Olson was one of the very few to actually read it, take some interest, and respond. And thank God he did. Because of him giving me the opportunity he did, he changed my life. Like I said, thank the good Lord."

Why did he choose Lute Olson as the coach to which to send his letters? "Obviously, I was aware of Coach Olson," he said. "I can always remember watching Arizona on television on weekend games. And it was so evident it was Arizona because of the cactus logo on the floor. I'll always remember the cactus logo. And I'll remember that Arizona was one of the best programs in America. He was one of the best coaches."

Pastner wanted to be one of the best coaches and learn from one of them in Olson. "I wanted to stay involved the game," Pastner said. "I still remember people talking like I was going to be the next Steve Kerr. But the reality was there was an opportunity to get there and learn...it worked itself out."

As for the letter, Olson responded and had then-assistant coach Jessie Evans reach out. Then, Pastner developed a relationship with coach Jim Rosborough, who eventually went to see him coach. As did Olson. At the time Pastner was coaching AAU ball, even though he wasn't older than 17. "As I look back, I think it was fascinating," he said. "You're in the moment of it. You're there coaching, and others are watching you coach. As I look back, it was really surreal to think about it."

Then Pastner joined the 1997 Arizona title team that featured Mike Bibby, Miles Simon, and Michael Dickerson. At the time few knew they'd be title contenders, but they were. "I knew my role," Josh said. "I had a clear understanding of what my opportunity was. I knew it early when I first got there. I realized it when we'd play in pickup games. And let me tell you: I worked on my game. I barely went to my senior prom because I worked so hard. Then you get to Arizona and you get the idea that you have a limit. And even if I would have never played, I would have soaked it all up, and it would not have affected me one bit."

Instead, he played in 42 games and was never part of a losing game. "It was great to have that experience," he said. "I remember we were highly ranked and we went to Louisiana State and played on a Saturday morning, and they just smashed us. It was my senior year. And we got punched. They kicked our rear, and the entire time I thought I'd get in, maybe to give our starters a rest."

Pastner never entered the game during that 86–60 loss. "My shoes were laced up tight, and for sure I thought I was getting in," he said. "The next morning when we were getting back on the plane to come back to Tucson—he was already on the plane and seated—he grabbed my arm with those huge hands. Those huge hands engulfed my entire arm, but he wanted to apologize to me...He apologized to me for not playing me in the game. He said, 'I wanted you to leave Arizona as an undefeated player so you can tell your kids and grandkids that you never went into a game that you lost.' He wanted me to leave undefeated. That was coming from his heart. I was kind of surprised that he even realized that."

Soon after—and months after Pastner kissed Lute & Bobbi Court to say good-bye to a career—Pastner was on Olson's coaching staff as a graduate assistant. "You know the entire time the guys would be my best friends and my great teammates, but I can't tell you how many times they'd say, 'Don't say this to Josh or do this or that because he'd go tell Coach O,'" Pastner said, laughing. "They'd look at me like I was going to go run to Coach. I'd tell them, 'Guys, no, that's not the case.' But you know my loyalties always ran with Coach, always. I was always looking to protect Coach Olson."

And that was all the time—as a player or as an assistant. "I still feel that to this day," Pastner said. "If anyone would say anything about Coach that wasn't positive, I was right there to defend him."

Olson was a cool customer, but he's still human. He could get heated after losses or after fans or media criticized him, especially opponents' fans. "I saw him get mad one time," Pastner said.

Josh Pastner (AP Images)

"You know that he never cursed or used foul language. You'd see him get angry or upset at the guys who did anything disrespectful. He did not tolerate that, and guys respected him out of fear, and I mean that in a good way. He didn't go out to hurt anyone or go out to make himself look bad. He demanded excellence. And the guys didn't want to disappoint him."

One incident in the Bay Area stood out. Arizona had just lost to Stanford and Cal in the final two games of the regular season just a week before the NCAA Tournament was to begin. Arizona was not at its best. "It was toward the end at the buzzer, and we just didn't get calls," Pastner recalled. "He felt we didn't play as hard as we should have, and we didn't. Then at the end, all of a sudden, the game is over, and here's this dad who came down from the stands with a kid on his shoulders screaming with vulgar language. The guy may have had too much to drink. Coach turned around to go at him. I'd never seen Coach do that. I thought he was going to go fight him. He caught himself right before the railing, walked back the other direction. It was the only time I saw him lose his cool."

There was the time when the players all wore headbands for a game against Washington State, a team Arizona had beaten more than 40 straight times. Arizona, one of the best teams in the country at the time, struggled to beat WSU at home, eventually winning 80–75. "Coach and Coach Roz knew about it," Pastner said. "I was going to wear one because I was a member of the team. I know the coaches were not in favor of it because they thought it would be a distraction."

Pastner said if they do wear the headbands, they'd better win the game by 30 or make it a blowout of some kind. "The guys got mad at me because I told the coaches, but I did it because, even though I was part of the team, I didn't want the coaches to get blindsided," he said. "I was wearing my coaching hat at the time. The coaches didn't say anything against it though."

Arizona struggled against WSU but eventually pulled it off. It helped that the players took off the headbands at halftime after struggling early. After the game Olson said the headbands "compressed their brains" because they played without intelligence. "Coach was very upset, very upset. It was good that we won the game. But we were bad. We were horrible," Pastner said. "Coach was not a happy camper, and that was to Coach's credit. This was one of his mottos: you drill the team when you are mad at them. But after a loss, their confidence is shaken so you're a little calmer on things. He stayed true to that. So when we won, he was harder on us after wins than losses."

Eventually, Pastner became part of Olson's staff after graduating—first as a graduate assistant, then video coordinator, and then a full-time assistant when Jay John took the head coaching job at Oregon State. Did rising up the ranks change his relationship with his mentor? "I don't know if it ever changed. Every time there was an opening of an assistant coach out there, he'd recommend me," Pastner said. "After 1998 I applied for this job or that job. I don't think he ever looked at me as a player. I think he looked at me as a coach the entire time because as a player I spent a lot of time with Coach Rosborough in the film room. I'd help with things. I'd rebound for the players as a student-athlete. I was there all the time. Then he'd have me look at player tendencies from opponents. How many times they went left? How many times they went right? He asked me to do that every game."

The transition to becoming a coach was easy. He eventually became a graduate assistant. And he was in the coach's meetings. "Once you're in there, it's kind of like sacred ground with the staff," he said. "What happens in there stays in there. He never told me that, but I knew. When I became a coach, it was amazing. He just brought me in and said, 'You want the job, and here's your pay.' I just jumped up and gave him a big hug around the neck. I think he was caught off guard because that wasn't him."

Pastner realized that so he said, "Sorry, Coach, I'm ready to go when you are. There was no rah-rah speech or anything. We just moved on to the next phase."

Soon, he was coaching the big men. A smallish guard—a walk-on, no less—was coaching the centers. "I was always down there with the bigs—even as a player helping. That was for Coach Johnson or Coach John. I was always there, never with the guards. Coach Olson always told me, 'You already know what's going on as a guard, but most guards don't know or aren't prepared to coach bigs.' He told me that when I was a freshman. He was master coach of the big men, an unbelievable coach with them. Everyone talks about his success with guards. He was unbelievable with the big men."

Eventually, after years at UA and a place many thought he'd stay forever, Pastner decided to leave for Memphis to be John Calipari's assistant coach. "It was really hard to leave," he said. "I had some other opportunities to be an assistant coach prior to that at other spots, but I wasn't ready to go. I didn't want to leave. At the time when Coach Calipari offered me the job to go to Memphis, I mean I was ready. I also at that time knew Coach was struggling. He eventually took a year off [for health reasons]."

Pastner could see Olson was starting to feel different. "I'd be in the locker room with him a lot," Pastner said. "It was hard to see Coach [struggle at times] because that's not the coach I knew, or we knew. The coach I knew was exercising every single day. He was strong. He was a walker. He walked a lot. He was extremely healthy, so to see him going through some of those health things he was going through was tough."

Eventually, Olson came back and was ready—seemingly—to lead UA again, but Pastner had taken the job at Memphis. "I wouldn't have gotten the job had I not gotten Coach Olson's blessing," Pastner said. "He was great about it. It allowed me to move to Memphis. Coach Olson said it was a great opportunity to learn from somebody else."

Eventually, Pastner was named head coach at Memphis after Calipari left for Kentucky. Pastner is now the head coach at Georgia Tech. Through all of the stops, he relied on things he learned from Olson. "Coach Olson is one of the great coaches ever in the history of sports," he said. "On top of that, he's an even better person. The positive impact he had on so many is immeasurable. Anyone who came in contact with Coach Olson knew it was an honor."

So, of course, he misses the man who had such a great impact on him as a player, coach, and person. "I miss him daily," Pastner said. "I love Coach. When people ask me about him, I filibuster about him. I can go on and on...I'm happy that he saw me become a head coach. I wish he could still be here. I get emotional when I think about him and what he did for me in my life. Because of one person's decision to allow me to be part of something has changed my life. Forget Josh Pastner—that's for countless people and not just players. And then consider the amount of charity work he did in the state and in Tucson and how he affected and influenced people in such a way. It's just remarkable."

13
Jim Rosborough

How does a person go from being a teacher and an eighth-grade boys basketball coach to being recognized as one of the country's best college basketball assistant coaches of the last 30 years? Good luck, happenstance, hard work, and doing the right things. Oh, being a good guy and meeting a man who eventually became a Hall of Fame basketball coach also help. "I was teaching school in Chicago on the west side in the spring of 1974," said Jim Rosborough, recalling how he met Lute Olson. "That spring, there was a kid playing out on the playground where I was teaching. I saw him. I can't remember his name, but he was not going anywhere [to college yet]. I had spoken to him. He was a good kid. One day I got on the phone and called Lute, who had just arrived at Iowa to coach."

Iowa was already set with recruits, but that was Rosborough's first conversation with Olson. Three or four months later, Iowa was looking for a third assistant coach. Rosborough's old coach, Sharm Scheuerman, who was the head coach at Iowa in the 1950s and early 1960s, connected the two. An interview was eventually set up and in stepped this "long-haired dude with crazy-ass sideburns" to meet Olson.

Of course, he wanted the job. "I didn't want to stay being an eighth-grade coach," Rosborough said. "We were pretty darn good, but I didn't want to stay. The job at Iowa was good. You could travel, you could recruit. The pay was awful but..."

But he was ready to take the job if offered. "Was I nervous? Sure, I was," he said. "I didn't know what to expect. There I was with bell-bottom pants. Yes, I'm an articulate guy and all that kind of crazy stuff, but as I related to him, I didn't know ball-side to help side."

But what Rosborough had going for him—and Olson recognized—was that Rosborough knew talent. More importantly, he knew Chicago talent. "And what Lute saw was that he had to get into Chicago to be successful," said Rosborough, who is nicknamed "Roz."

And, well, that was Roz's background—knowing the talent in Chicago. He was born there and had been back for eight years. Of course, Roz got hired. "I had no idea what I was getting into," Roz said.

Two days into settling down, Roz was out recruiting. He'd come back and meet with Olson and the other assistants. What he discovered was what others either already knew or eventually found out—Olson was pretty good at what he did. "I quickly found out I had to get back in [Chicago] to meet the coaches and talk to the kids," he said. "We had to have an immediate turn-around. So, we just jumped in without a life preserver and got after it. That's how it was. I do remember coming out of meetings and the staff saying, 'That was one of the best meetings ever.' This guy was a detail-oriented guy. We covered everything. We talked about everything we'd teach. It was absolutely amazing."

Jim Rosborough
(left) and Gilbert
Arenas (AP Images)

Through it all early in his coaching career, Roz remembered the sound advice of his father: "Work so hard they can't get rid of you."

Olson knew what he had in Roz: a guy he could depend on who was a hard worker and had an eye for talent. "I'm not sure he knew what he was getting into either," Roz said. "He had been a Division I coach for a year and a junior college coach before that. Yes, he had this vision, and there wasn't a question about his ability. But we were jumping into the Big Ten. As I look back, it had so much talent. One game we played Indiana, and they beat us 102–49. The league was phenomenal. But he was a fast learner. We started getting better kids."

Given his status as a coaching luminary, was Olson intimidating? "I wouldn't say that" Roz said. "I would say he was more of a father type, a guy who worked so we worked. We'd go into the office at 7:00 and we'd be cranking it hard in the early days."

They went to all the clinics to meet coaches. They were everywhere in Chicago. In the first year, Iowa went 10–16, and it seemed tough. "We'd see Bobbi and him walking off the floor, and he looked like all the blood was gone from his face," he said. "It wasn't fun in the first year. Well, it was fun to a degree, but we just didn't have players and we weren't winning."

Iowa then went 19–10 and 20–7 in back-to-back years after that. Eventually, Iowa made it to the Final Four in 1980 with four of the top six players from Chicago. Iowa hadn't been to the Final Four since 1955. Roz was promoted to be the top assistant whose duties were working on campus. "I was not named associate head coach, but I was dealing with all the on-campus stuff," he said. "He liked my attention to detail, and I had done a good job within the athletic department with the academics and all that kind of stuff."

That year of the Final Four, Roz was already doing most of the scouting reports while being assisted by Tony McAndrews, who earlier in the season was in a plane crash that limited him. Roz was also assisted by Ken Burmeister, another future Arizona assistant. "He had confidence in what I was doing," Roz said. "If there was a big game or a tournament game, I'd be the main scout. It carried over to Arizona. He knew I could look at film and be confident in what I saw."

So, for years there were few people who spent more time with Lute than Roz—other than Bobbi and his family. Roz was his trusted assistant. Did he ever see the buttoned-down coach lighten up? "There were times," he said, laughing. "We'd get together with friends and stuff like that. No question there were good times. We met Bobbi, and I had eventually met Kim [Roz's wife]. Bobbi was really nice, and they got along. We saw their family grow. Our family was growing. So, yes, there were lighter times. We took a [team] trip to South America, and that was a lot of fun. We met great people. And I think they had wine down there. But we had a good time."

They had a good time, but overall it was more of a business relationship. "I wouldn't say we hung out all the time," Roz said. "We did a little bit off the floor but not a lot. It was about working and producing and trusting one another."

In addition to becoming Olson's right-hand man, Roz was becoming one of the best assistant coaches in the Midwest. Olson knew his value. "We'd drive to and from Chicago and just have good conversations," he said. "He understood from an external standpoint what I was doing. He trusted me in recruiting. He knew that I knew what I was doing."

Roz ran his camps. One year he had 28 Division I players in attendance. "It was unbelievable," he said. "We had Kenny Arnold, Randy Brewer, and more."

After nine years with Olson at Iowa—and five NCAA appearances—Roz eventually left for Tulsa for a year and then became the head coach at Northern Illinois for three years. He was let go from NIU, and Olson called to bring him to Arizona after Kevin O'Neill left to take the Marquette job. "At the time I was hired, he was taking his team to Europe, and I didn't go. I stayed to run his camp, which I had done all these years for him at Iowa," Roz said. "Things went smoothly. It was like nothing had changed, just different players and setting. It was a real easy transition for him."

Things, though, had changed on one front. The programs were entirely different. When Roz returned in 1989–90, he realized Arizona was not Iowa. "Arizona was pretty well-established," he said. "They'd recently been to the Final Four, and there were good players: Harvey Mason, Sean Rooks, Matt Muehlebach, Matt Othick, and the rest. I got here and recognized pretty quickly they needed to stay at the high level they were at. It was a nationally recognized program, top 20 almost every single year from then on."

The biggest differences, however, were the locker rooms and perhaps the mood of the team. "When we were at Iowa, the locker room was kind of staid and beat up. There was not much music. We just got ready to play," he said. "I get to Arizona, and it's looser. It was more of a cool atmosphere. There was music in there but not blared. The kids were a little more relaxed…The thing I realized was it was going to be tough to stay at the top. And we needed to keep it there. So recruiting was crucial, and coaching them was critical."

NCAA Tournament appearances continued. Arizona returned to the Final Four in 1994 and won it all in 1997. With Arizona having reached the top perch, did anything change with Olson? "He was out in public a little bit more, out to lunch with boosters," he said. "He'd work in the morning, then go to lunch. That didn't happen a lot in Iowa, at least not with boosters so much. I would say he was a little bit looser, but again if he was out doing stuff, then things had to be done in the office, and they were. He trusted it was going to be done well because it had been done well. There was no real big change other than he became a bigger personality in the community. There had been the 1988 Final Four and the first No. 1 ranking, Sean Elliott, and a bunch of great kids. And he was the same coach—attention to detail, tough, demanding, ask that they play hard."

Olson enjoyed being the face of the community for the most part. "Partly yes," he said. "There's that notoriety. It's like being a movie star. I think he liked it a little bit. Come on, how many coaches do you know who don't have an ego? Did he like being Lute? Sure."

Roz said traveling to away games with the Wildcats was like going on the road with "rock stars." "We pull into the Madison Square Garden, we'd pull up to Vegas," he said, "and fans were there. It was like The Rolling Stones coming in. The coverage was huge, Dick Vitale, ESPN, Digger Phelps, everyone. It was amazing, and he was the centerpiece. So, yes, I think he liked it.

You have to have a little ego. I never saw that as a staff. But yeah, I think he loved being Lute."

Shortly after the 1997 national championship, Olson named Roz the team's associate head coach. "I mean, I was very pleased," Roz said. "I was surprised and kind of emotional there for about a minute. Things didn't really change, just the title."

Eventually, Arizona returned to the Final Four in 2001. But not before some heartache. Olson's wife of more than 40 years passed away on New Year's Day in 2001, and Olson stepped away for about two weeks, leaving Roz in charge. "That was a tough year, really tough," Roz said. "There was a point there when he came down to practice to tell the team he'd be gone, and that she was not going to make it. That was horrible, and you're trying to keep the kids together, get them ready for games."

Roz won three of four games, and then Olson came back. "We just rolled, but that was a good team," he said, "probably the most talent that's ever been there—position by position and bench. It'll tell you when we're not even starting Luke Walton… But her death affected a lot of people. My wife was good friends. We were good friends with their children. We just kept doing our jobs."

Arizona eventually made it to the national championship game, losing to Duke 82–71 in Minneapolis. Six years—and many victories—later, Olson decided to change assistant coaches, bringing back O'Neill to replace Roz, who had been asked to take a different position with the team. He declined. So after 18 years at Arizona and nine at Iowa, Roz was out. "Everything was fine," Roz said. "It was the last 10 minutes [of that coaching relationship] that wasn't. I didn't have any idea at all what was happening. I didn't know what he was going to do. Eventually, he asked me to get off the court and stop coaching."

Roz stood up and said, "I'm not doing it. I walked out and packed up my stuff on a Sunday, and that was it. It was unpleasant, and I still don't know exactly his reasoning or thinking was on that."

Conversations—if any—were rare afterward. O'Neill then took over as an interim coach, taking the team to the NCAA Tournament after what was another difficult year as Olson stepped away because of health reasons. There had been problems with O'Neill and his difficult style. O'Neill had a rough season and ruffled a lot of players in the program. Olson later returned, but O'Neill did not.

Then a phone conversation between Olson and Roz ensued. "I put in a call—because everyone knew there were problems in the program with Kevin—to say to Lute, 'Maybe we can talk and work something out to get this going for another couple of years,'" Roz said.

Olson agreed. They met, and the first thing out of Olson's mouth was: did you know about the situation with O'Neill? "We met, and there wasn't even a hello," Roz said. "I said, 'Coach, everybody in the country did.' So, we then we shook hands. We had breakfast another day, and he said, 'Yep, I'm gonna go down and get this taken care of [and bring you back]' and shook hands, and that's the last day…well, I never really spoke to him again."

Their conversation occurred in 2007. Olson then took a leave of absence for 2007–08 before retiring in 2008.

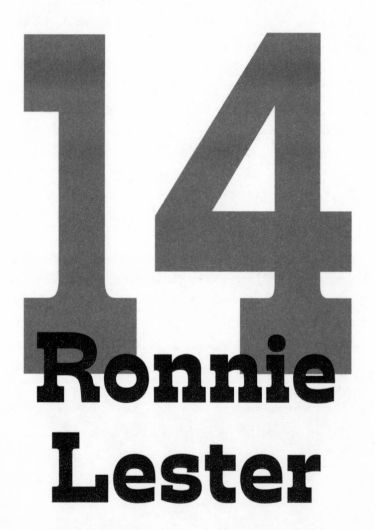

14
Ronnie
Lester

Ronnie Lester, the cat-quick guard at Iowa, helped Lute Olson get to the Final Four for the first time back in 1980. They helped build a program from 1974 to 1983. Lester was in the middle of all that—and perhaps the centerpiece of the resurgence of Hawkeye basketball.

His first contact with Iowa was through Tony McAndrews, who was with Olson for a number of years at Iowa and Arizona while Lester was in his senior year in Chicago. At the time Lester "knew nothing" about Olson. But McAndrews and Olson started to show up at games and practices. The more they saw, the more they were impressed.

The feeling was mutual. "Coach Olson was always so professional," Lester said. "He handled himself really, really well. That's the thing I remember about Coach Olson: how professional he was and how regal he was."

Before making a decision on where to attend college, Lester set up his visits. He visited the University of Arizona when Fred Snowden was the coach. The others were Nebraska, Creighton, and Iowa. "It was the month of May," he said. "And Coach Olson wanted me to make Iowa the last visit."

Before that chance to make the final impression, Olson and a couple of coaches made an in-home visit. "He met my mom and my three sisters, and they all fell in love with him and the coaching staff," he said. "They just didn't recruit me but my whole family—my mom and sisters. They wanted me to go to Iowa because of the relationship they had started with Coach Olson and his coaching staff."

Of course they did. Many—if not all the players—said their moms loved Olson as did Lester's, but there was also something else. "He was always so professional," he said. "He knew how to treat people. He was just a special person first and foremost. In talking to Coach Olson, while he was recruiting me, I told him I wanted to go someplace where I thought I could play right away. I didn't want to sit for a year. He promised me I would get a chance to play. I remember him telling me that he couldn't promise me I'd start but that I'd get a chance to play. He did say that if I went to Iowa, I'd get my degree and that he'd make me a better player. You know coaches tell you a lot of different things. I was offered some inducements to go to a different school, which I didn't do. I wanted to play for Coach Olson and his staff."

He signed with Iowa, and the future looked bright. But he was also this kid from inner-city Chicago now in Iowa City, a smallish town for a kid from the big city. "It was tough...the first couple of months," Lester said. "I get to the university, and I'm 17 years old. It's so different than what I'm used to. I've got different teammates, and the atmosphere is different."

The first couple of months were more about about going to class and getting acclimated to the lifestyle of school rather than basketball. That wasn't great because he wanted to play. "I would call my mother almost every night, telling her I want to come home," he said. "I was homesick. She had to talk me out of it.

The big thing was I had no way to get back home. That was probably the biggest hindrance [to leaving]."

Basketball practice—or at least working out—then started in October, and he got to play in pick-up games. "It got better, but I probably would have left if I had a way to go," he said.

He never spoke to Olson about being homesick.

The first year, Iowa finished 18–9, and Lester played in every game. They finished third in the Big Ten—an improvement from fifth the year before. "I don't think any of the experts thought we'd do well," he said. "We were always picked to finish at the bottom of the conference. My first year was a surprise to people. It was a good year. We thought we had a chance to go to the NIT after the season. But we didn't get picked."

By the time Lester was a junior and then senior, Iowa was one of the best teams in the conference. In 1978 Iowa tied for the league title. Then Iowa was good enough his senior year to get to the Final Four. Iowa finished fourth in the conference after Lester, who was leading the team in scoring at 14.3 points per game, suffered a knee injury early in the season. He later came back at the end of the regular season. He helped Iowa get through the early rounds in the NCAA tournament before suffering another injury in the semifinal game of the Final Four against Louisville, the eventual champion.

He remembered Olson being consistent throughout the highs and lows of his Iowa tenure. "He's always pretty much the same," he said. "He straightforward. He's aboveboard. Whether you're winning or losing, it's always the same. The thing I loved about him and playing for him was he always scripted out the practices. He had an itinerary for every minute. If we were going to do something, he had it written down on a piece of paper. We'd cover certain things every minute of every practice. He was always so detailed, so well-prepared."

He said he took some of Olson's qualities to heart. "I learned a lot from my different coaches," he said. "When I first got to Iowa, I didn't really know Coach. I just knew his persona. After playing for him, you got to know him a little bit. He became more than just a coach. You could see him juggling so many hats. He was not only a basketball coach. He was a father and a husband. He was a man of faith. You saw all those things in his daily life. You would see him with his family...all the time. He was going to church on Sundays, all those things, those qualities that you see in a person you'd like to rub off on you. He was doing the right things the right way."

Olson was almost like a surrogate father to Lester. "I grew up in a home without a father. My mother raised me and my three sisters," he said. "My father figures to me were always coaches I played for. So you try to take something positive from every coach. They become the role models you're around. Coach Olson had a lot of positive things about him."

One thing he obviously noticed was Olson's demeanor. Olson was stoic, never really showing his emotions like a good poker player. He had this gift of convincing his players they were good, and they were. "He was like a flatline yet always upbeat especially with us," he said. "He was always confident. I think he knew that. He had to be that way for us to have confidence in ourselves. He was always that way. We went into every game thinking we had a chance to win because of Coach Olson. It was the way about him. We felt that if we worked as hard as anybody else, we had as good a chance to win just as any other team. Coach always gave us that confidence to go out there and play."

Lester enjoyed being around Olson, but it was a player-coach relationship—not a friendship. "He knew where to draw the line. He was not going to be buddy, buddy with you. He had a job to do as a coach," Lester said. "But you loved him. You had a great love and respect for him. The things he did were always very respectful. I look back on the coaches that I played for, and he's definitely right at the top."

That's saying a lot given Lester played for some notable coaches with the Chicago Bulls (Jerry Sloan, Rod Thorn, and Paul Westhead) and the Los Angeles Lakers (Pat Riley). Throughout Lester's pro career, Olson and Lester would stay in contact, talking every once in a while. Lester became a scout and assistant general manager with the Lakers and visited Arizona to scout UA's players. His post-college life created a new dynamic between coach and former player. "It's not like we weren't friendly [at Iowa], but we became more friendly later," he said. "I knew Coach's family because you'd always see him with the family and I had spent time with them at his home. He'd always be concerned with how you were not just as a player but as a person, too. He'd want to know what was going on in your life. If you needed help and he could help, he'd try to in any type of way. He valued your friendship. He became a friend to me."

They have a bond since they were so integral to Iowa basketball in the late 1970s and early 1980s. Olson became a major figure in that region. "Iowa is a small state and was smaller back then," Lester said. "There are no professional sports in the state, so they really get behind college athletics there. When Coach turned the program around, he really got things going. He was like a rock star just as he was at Arizona. In Iowa I don't think he could go many places and not be noticed. Everyone in the state knew who he was. I think he handled it well, even though there were a lot of demands on him. They loved him."

Lester is very glad that he chose to play for Olson at Iowa. "I learned so much from him," he said. "He treated people as you'd want to be treated—with respect. Those are the things I take away from him. Eventually, he became not so much a coach to me but an important role model. I imagined doing some of the things I saw in him. Going to Iowa was a lot of fun. I look back on those days and making the decision to go to Iowa to play for Coach Olson and I know I couldn't have made a better decision. It was because of him."

15
Craig McMillan

ute Olson called the recruitment of Craig McMillan crucial. When McMillan decided to commit and sign with UA back in the mid-1980s, it gave Arizona its first McDonald's All-American. He was the start of good things to come since he was the first of what is now about 30 All-Americans. "I remember him starting to recruit me the summer before my senior year at a Vegas tournament," McMillan said. "It was likely I started getting letters in the spring from him, and then it picked up in the summer."

McMillan remembered it was the first year that recruits could sign in the early signing period, which would have meant early winter. "I did not sign in November because I wanted to wait," he said. "Arizona had been so far down I didn't want to commit right away. I wanted to see what type of progress it was going to make that first year."

It took a while, but Arizona did make progress, going 11–17 in Olson's first year at Arizona. The key was it won five of its last seven games. Remember: Arizona was 4–24 the year before Olson got to Arizona. Still, it was a big risk for a McDonald's All-American to take a chance on a program that had seen little success to that point. "They convinced me and explained that Coach and his staff were going to do well and that they'd be a success. And they proved it," he said. "They sold it with that success at the end of the season."

The success wasn't a surprise. McMillan, from Cloverdale, California, is the son of a coach. And he knew what good coaching entailed. "Everybody into college basketball knew who Lute was and his success at Iowa," he said. "Then, I learned more during the recruiting process...Just the type of person he was more than anything. I think what people respected most about Coach Olson was his discipline and camaraderie and unselfishness. He just didn't talk about it. He actually promoted it. He talked about not having morons on the team or players who acted crazy. He didn't want any of that."

And he was a pretty good recruiter. "He sent me a postcard with a McKale Center photo on it," McMillan said. "And he said on the card, 'It will probably be called McMillan Center after you're done at Arizona.'"

Smooth.

McMillan did not get the stadium named after him. He, however, got a shot named after him. The McShot came when he picked up a deflected cross-court pass from Steve Kerr in a 63–62 overtime win against Oregon State.

But when McMillan arrived, he received something else, something he wasn't expecting. "He was a guy with Midwestern values. It was about discipline on and off the court, people having to act the right way," McMillan said. "He wasn't just concerned about the performance of the team, but he was concerned about how everybody acted and behaved in addition to how they progressed as individuals on and off the court."

Off-the-court responsibilities were important, and there was some pressure to be good all the time for these teenagers. "There was a little bit. He always wanted to give back to the community, have players go into schools and speak to people, read to the younger kids, and you had to do some of that regularly, which [some] didn't really like at the time," McMillan said. "But after the fact, you realize how important it is."

McMillan made an impact right away, being the first player off the bench as a freshman. He played behind veterans Brock Brunkhorst and Kerr. It was playing time he earned. "I wouldn't have respected a coach had he made any kind of promises," he said. "I'd say my dad [as a high school coach] had the same old-school values, and anyone that's promising you time, my dad and I would not have been interested in."

In fact, Olson reminded him of his father. "In a lot of ways," he said, "there were a lot of similarities. They emphasized fundamentals, discipline, work ethic, toughness, all that—the old-school things that are important to be successful."

And that emphasis started from the first practice of the season for McMillan, who was part of Olson's second class at UA. "The first practice a year before was a little tougher because when he got there he found out or realized they were farther behind than he thought," McMillan said. "I heard it was something like four hours. But I also think he was setting the tone of where they were, where they are, and where they needed to get to. I think the media guide said it all when the coaches and players were wearing hard hats, and it was a complete reconstruction. I think that helped people know that the expectations needed to be realistic...We had a lot of conditioning and stuff."

Through these practices McMillan realized how meticulous Olson was. Practice was to the minute. Drills had to be done correctly. And then, well, there were the sheets he used to grade players. "He was ahead of his time, analytical, performance charts," he said. "And the game has evolved."

When McMillan started his coaching career—he's now the longtime head coach at Santa Rosa Junior College—he used the same performance sheets. "We've changed it a little bit but

Craig McMillan (Courtesy Craig McMillan)

not much," he said. "We use it in our practices to evaluate the players. We post them after practice just to show the guys a little more accountability."

By 1987–88 Arizona was the talk of the town, the state of Arizona, and parts of the nation. The Wildcats were beating teams by double digits and enjoying every part of it. UA had reached No. 1 on December 28, 1987. It then reached the Final Four for the first time in school history four months later. "It was a great run. What an amazing experience," McMillan said. "We were playing so well so when we lost to Oklahoma. It was tough to swallow."

How did Olson take it? "He was very upset," he said. "Everybody's emotional after the game, and it was tough, just tough. It was particularly hard for me being a senior and knowing that was my last chance. If you were an underclassman, you knew you'd have another chance, so it was easier for them to take. But I'd say he was probably as crushed as I had ever seen him. At the time that's as close as we'd ever been to winning a national championship. So, it was tough."

Then came what many thought was a classic moment for Olson—or at least another side to the stoic, regal coach that everyone saw on a day-to-day basis. It came at the post-Final Four party in front of thousands of fans at Arizona Stadium. On the stage with his players, Olson started dancing alongside his players for a song. "We just had a phenomenal season, and the fans were supporting the way we played. It was amazing," McMillan said. "It was a great celebration but still kind of bitter-sweet after having lost…His public persona is a little bit different and sometimes a little looser than he portrays sometimes."

Once McMillan was out of school, it was different. It's consistent with what others have said about Olson. The relationship changes from coach to mentor to friend. Once Olson retired in the later 2000s, he had more time to enjoy his life. A great way was to join McMillan, Joe Turner, and others on McMillan's boat in the Bay Area. About 10 years ago, Kelly Olson (Lute's wife) said her husband loved joining the guys. There had been invitations before but nothing formal. "The first year he came up here was the best fishing we had ever had," McMillan said. "It was just phenomenal. We got all kinds of salmon, lots of it. I think he came back about four or five times."

McMillan said he had the time of his life. There were no worries. It was a side of Olson, though, McMillan had seen before over the years and that he enjoyed seeing again. "When he would go fishing, he would want to go out first thing in the morning and would want to stay out as long as he could. He never wanted to come back [to shore]," McMillan said. "Tom [Tolbert] would be getting seasick, and everybody else would be getting tired. But Coach wanted to stay out there as long as we possibly could."

Olson was quite the fisherman. "He was very good, very good for not having done that type of fishing," McMillan said. "We were kind of half joking, but during that first trip, he was up here asking all kinds of questions first. And then after about a day, he's like, 'Great, let's go here and there by the rocks'...telling us where we should go."

It was particularly special for McMillan, who also was able to have him in his element. "That was really cool having him up there," he said. "One year we were having a basketball camp, so he came by and spoke to the camp. It was very good. The kids weren't as impressed as the parents were."

Of course they were. They were hearing a living legend—a Hall of Fame basketball coach—talk to their kids. And when Olson spoke, people listened. They learned the same things McMillan had known since arriving on campus that fall of 1984. "I learned countless basketball nuances obviously," he said. "And it's a continuation of what my parents taught me, the values your parents teach you: to be a good person, take care of your responsibilities, be unselfish, everything in moderation."

McMillan called those "special" times. He also enjoyed seeing him in the later years, when he came to visit for the Lute Olson Fantasy Camp. "It was good, [but] it was hard to see people when they aren't able to do the things they used to do," he said. "But seeing him was always great. It was great to see him as much as we did in the last few years."

And, of course, he misses him. "Someone who has been part of your life for that long, of course, you're going to miss," McMillan said.

16
Matt Muehlebach

It was the mid-1980s, and Matt Muehlebach already had started following Lute Olson's Arizona teams. Not only was he already a Pac-10 fan, but his mom also was originally from Iowa. "I'm not sure anything had really jumped off the page early, but I do know they were pretty solid his first two or three years," Muehlebach said. "I remember watching them in the NCAA Tournament, and they had lost their first-round games to Auburn, then Alabama."

That was one reason he had another school—besides Arizona—in his mind at first. "It's not like that was the school I wanted to go to," he said. "I always wanted to go to Stanford."

But then he started watching Sean Elliott, Steve Kerr, and others and saw the improved results. Arizona soon impressed him by winning its first Pac-10 title. "I saw what Lute was doing and could tell how it was starting to become a pretty good thing," he said.

His initial preference of Stanford—along with Kansas and Arizona—were in the mix for his services until he stepped on the Arizona campus. "When I went to make my visit," he said, "that sealed it for me."

He said Olson, of course, played a "huge factor" in him ultimately enrolling at Arizona. "He was the main reason I picked

Arizona," he said. "If Lute wasn't there, I don't go to Arizona—not even close. Of course, there were other things I liked about Arizona, but if he's not there, there is no discussion...You could feel his energy toward making Arizona a national power, and he just had a presence. He had this confidence [and] belief in what in what he was doing, and I loved how he coached. He had a mix of different players."

Muehlebach remembers seeing a sign in the Arizona locker room that said: "No one plays harder, no one players smarter, no one plays more together." Muehlebach said. "I could tell he appreciated players who played hard and played as a team."

Olson wasn't about recruiting the best player in the country. Instead it had to be a player who fit the program. It had to be the right kind of player. "When I got to Arizona, it was like, yeah, these are my guys," he said. "This is like Joe Turner, Steve Kerr, Sean Elliott, Tom Tolbert...I didn't need to go anywhere else because he was building this basketball power. It's corny to say, but he was also building a family, too."

It indeed was like a family, but Muehlebach actually got closer to Olson later in life. "I also want to emphasize that he wasn't the Lute I got to know 20 years later, " he said. "There was a clear separation between him and I. I knew he appreciated how I played. And I knew he was confident in me. But it wasn't like we were best buddies. I rarely talked to him."

Muehlebach relayed an incident at McKale Center when he was with a friend. "I told my friend: 'Watch me mess with Lute,'" Muehlebach said. "'Hey, Coach, how are you doing?' Coach looked at me like, *Why are you talking to me?*"

It wasn't that Olson treated Muehlebach unfairly or with indifference, but there was a clear hierarchy with Kerr, Elliott, and Craig McMillan at the top. "There was a definite sense to earn your stripes," he said, "before you got any sort of status."

Muehlebach said he and the other underclassmen found the practices to be intense. "It was not easy early on," he said, "[like] playing against the No. 1 team in the nation. You got it handed

Matt Muehlebach (Courtesy Steve Lavin)

to you every day. Heck, I was going against Craig McMillan, who was 6'6", 220 pounds. He was a man who could have played in the NBA. It was tough. It reminds me of doing jujitsu or something like that. They get pinned 700 times before they move up in belts. That's what it felt like. You had to fail constantly, but you had to fight through it. Those were tough times."

But that was the method to Olson's madness: you got better by playing people who were better than you. And as you got better, the team got better. "I've said this a thousand times...he's an incredible player development coach," Muehlebach said. "He coached the fundamentals and the understanding of the game. We played a ton, and he thrived on competition. Even in drills he did that. It was competition from minute one, and he ended every practice with a scrimmage. It may have been a 10-minute one or a 90-minute one, but there was one because he loved the competition...competing and winning were at the top of his recruiting checklist."

Those scrimmages and practices improved Muehlebach as a person and player. "It was a constant battle of failure and then trying to get better," he said. "I'm not sure they used this phrase back then, but you had to have this really high 'emotional intelligence' because you had to really work through it."

Muehlebach said he heard a famous line from former UA player Mark Georgeson, who eventually transferred, while stretching to get ready for a practice. He said, "You know what? I'm not even worried about today's practice. I'm already worried about tomorrow's."

The reserves behind Bruce Fraser were nicknamed the Gumbies because of all the abuse they'd take from the starters.

Bendable, malleable but dependable. "Our roles were pretty defined, and I knew I wasn't going to play a lot of games, but we were winning by a lot," he said. "The scout team would get beat up every day. Yes, we thought it was funny being the Gumbies, but it was more like a survival and a way to cope for not playing because it sucked not playing. Every player, who doesn't play, knows what I'm talking about. It sucks—and even when you're winning, and we were winning a lot."

But things started to click when Muehlebach and the others were able to be the opponents while on scout team games. During one scrimmage Muehlebach played the role of Iowa star B.J. Armstrong and "had the shooting day of my lifetime."

Then it happened again. "Then I could tell Lute felt I could play," he said. "I got the respect of the other players. Once I started playing like that, I knew I could play at that level. It took me a couple of months."

Later in his career, things got easier. No question it was still hard, but it was easier. He played more and eventually became a captain. Heck, he also became the winningest Wildcats player in the program, being part of 110 victories in his career. That impressive number wasn't surpassed until Dusan Ristic in 2018. Muehlebach is still the only Arizona player (who played more than one year) to go undefeated in the McKale Center. He was not only successful, but also a team leader. "It was great. I always wanted that, and in some ways, you might think it would get harder because of the responsibility, but in some ways, it got a lot easier," he said. "He was able to coach you more like someone who belonged or someone in the inner circle. He might still get on you. That didn't go away, but he could go to battle with you."

By this time if he had wanted to say, "Hey, Coach" from across the McKale Center, Olson would have responded.

Olson, though, still had his routines. He loved his pregame walks. He loved his hand-written, to-the-minute practice schedules. He always ate pregame popcorn. Muehlebach watched and learned. He took it all in and still uses some of the same philosophies Olson had. "One hundred percent I do," he said. "Two of the biggest things are organization and preparation. He was a master at preparation. And in whatever you're in—whatever business you are in or whatever you do—you have to be the best. And in order to be the best, you have to be incredibly prepared. I witnessed his passion for what he did."

Later in Olson's life, Muehlebach was with him for a nice steak dinner at a friend's house, but Olson insisted on listening to the Arizona State–Washington game on the radio. "I said, 'Coach, neither team is even in the Pac-10 race,'" Muehlebach told him. "'And it's on the radio. What are you going to learn from it on the radio? It's not like you're watching it to scout them.' But it was him and very telling for me to just understand his passion for what he was doing and his commitment to it at such a deep level. He just poured his whole self into it. I saw the energy—both mentally and physically—it took for him to be good."

The other quality Muehlebach took from Olson was his love and appreciation for fundamentals. "You can use that in anything in life—business or whatever it is," Muehlebach said. "You'd have to kind of understand the fundamentals of things before you do anything."

Muehlebach often talks about a game in Pittsburgh in the early 1990s where Arizona arrived late into the city and had an early game the next day. It was cold, and Arizona players were tired from the travel. So that the players could get their blood flowing, Olson told the team to be up early for one of his routine walks. Of course, the team was tired and didn't want to go. At the time Muehlebach was a captain. So he spoke to assistant coach Jim Rosborough to see if the team could skip the walk. The request was made, but Olson would have nothing of it. The team had to be there—or else. "The request went over like a turd in a punchbowl," Muehlebach joked. "There were no shortcuts with him…That was his approach."

By the time Muehlebach became a top attorney in Tucson, he was already good friends with Olson. They'd see each other from time to time. It was strange, odd, and cool. "All of those because I didn't expect it," he said. "But it was really cool. It was cool from the standpoint of we've been through those battles together. It's an unwritten connection that unless you're in them you can't really feel it, those unwritten connections of being in those battles, having practices after we lost games, that feeling where every loss felt like five losses. Those losses felt like the world was going to end and then being in those incredible successes. We won the Pac-12 four times in a row. We won the Pac-12 Tournament three times in a row, but there were failures. We never won the national title. But the higher you go up in the pyramid, the failures became life-altering things. I still think about them to this day, and it's tough. But that's what also makes the journey so much sweeter."

Having gone through the ups and downs together, Muehlebach and Olson became close. Team get-togethers were always fun. At one basketball reunion, many of the players eventually met up at Olson's house before they were scheduled to go see a football game at Arizona Stadium. "We were all getting ready to go to the game after having a great time," he said. "We had dinner, drinks, all that, great time. People started to leave for the game. Some guys stayed—Kerr, Elliott, Fraser, others—and watched the game at Lute's house. It was incredible. We were sitting there with Lute having a good time. We said, 'Do we really want to go?' We didn't leave. We sat on his balcony telling stories, having fun, talking smack to one another. Lute loved it. He could not have been happier. It was like he was a little kid. His guys were there with him. We wanted to hang with him rather than go to the game. It was awesome."

Another get-together occurred when one of the players was getting married, and they ended up having some fun at Olson's house. Many of the former players were there, eventually finding their way into the jacuzzi. "The temperature of the water wasn't right, and Lute didn't know how to work the jacuzzi, couldn't get the heat right," Muehlebach said. "[Fraser] yelled out, 'Coach, get to know your house! Get to know your things around here, Coach.' He was making fun of him. He had no idea how to work it. Heck, that was the last thing on his list to know. Coach laughed."

Like those other players, Muehlebach misses his former coach/ friend. "He was the reason why I went to UA," Muehlebach said. "He was the reason why I have so many great friends and experiences and life experiences and opportunities. It's tough not to have him around."

17
Reggie Geary

It was Las Vegas, and Reggie Geary was playing in a high school game when Lute Olson made his presence known. He was interested in the then-sophomore. "That kind of got my attention," Geary said. "Then I started getting letters and postcards."

Yes, of course, he was excited. Here was *the* coach of the University of Arizona looking to recruit the guard from Mater Dei, a well-known basketball program under Gary McKnight. "I was nervous for sure and, yes, excited," he said. "The big schools back then were UNLV, UCLA, and Arizona. It was definitely exciting."

For a 16 year old back then, he could sense Olson's aura. "When you're that young, you don't know the full story...like I didn't know that he had taken Iowa to the Final Fours and things of that nature," Geary said. "I just knew he was the head coach of one of the top programs. And as I got to know him more, I realized he was larger than life. It's just his presence. It was everything about him. He was very, very impressive. He was more impressive than Jim Harrick walking into your room. And, of course, Coach McKnight had a liking and great respect for him."

Parents loved him, too. "My dad was very impressed, became an instant fan as soon as he met the man," he said. "On his visit everything lined up perfect."

In fact, it seemed like Geary was a perfect fit for Arizona given the history at Mater Dei. McKnight taught the same principles as Olson and stressed the fundamentals. Geary kind of already knew the Arizona Way. "I remember Chris Mills, on the first day of practice, saying, 'You already know the drills.' I think that's why Coach O took a liking to me," Geary said. "He did have a lot of confidence in me from very early on. I knew I had his attention and I wanted to keep it."

Arizona had Mills, Damon Stoudamire, Khalid Reeves, and the rest of them. It had been to a Final Four not long before and was No. 1 for most of the 1989 season. Of course, Arizona had been in the NCAA Tournament all those previous years too. "All that took my full attention," Geary said. "Coach was a big part of that. He created that environment. You knew it was a big-time program. I never in my four years lost that feeling that this wasn't a big-time, blue-blood program. I knew you needed to come to work every day. You did not want to disappoint Coach. You didn't want to disappoint your teammates. That's how I went about it."

That's what Olson wanted. He wanted his players to play hard for the coaches, play hard for their teammates, play hard for their school, and play hard for themselves. That's how you got better in a very intense atmosphere. "There was so much competition," Geary said. "If you didn't perform, there was somebody right behind you. They were either pushing you or ready to take your place. It was that competitive environment that he created. It was a healthy competitiveness. It was never a negative thing. Coaches encouraged the competition. He also wanted us to play our game and do what we do. That made us productive. I played my second game and started a couple my freshman year. But I also knew the next year I'd have Michael Dickerson and Miles [Simon] coming in, and it would be competitive. He just created a great environment for guys to come in and compete, and if you did well, he'd reward you."

It's how Arizona built its reputation. The other players on the roster made each other better and prepared them for the NBA. "For sure," Geary said. "What a blessing to have a coach like that. And he was a Hall of Fame recruiter, too. It must have been fun to do that. Coach had a great eye for recruiting talent. He had great players in front of him and got answers every practice. It made games easy."

There were, however, tough games, too. Arizona went through first-round losses in the 1992 and 1993 NCAA Tournaments. Geary was a senior in high school in 1992 and a freshman in 1993. But then in 1994, it came together for UA to get to its first Final Four since 1988. "It was great…a magical year," Geary said. "Anytime you get to a Final Four and have a championship year, it's great. Maybe it's a little bit of rose-colored glasses as I look back, but the year was really smooth. We had just gone through a tough time the year before."

That was when Olson re-invented himself again. Going from what was a bigger lineup to a smaller, stealthier one behind Reeves, Stoudamire, Geary, Joseph Blair, Ray Owes, and others, UA ran through its opponents, going 29–6. To prepare for the season, UA went on an overseas summer trip, following the previous year's disappointing, first-round loss to Santa Clara. "Luckily for us, we got to go to Australia," Geary said. "We got to get out of the country, getting away from all our worries. It wasn't like we were running away because it was a scheduled trip. We got to re-bond. We got to smile again. Coach now started a three-guard offense. We were having fun with Joseph Blair, Ray Owes. Khalid and Damon were doing their thing. It kind of got that Santa Clara loss off us and into a good place…We came back refreshed and ready to go."

Geary called the trip a "godsend," and it culminated with the Final Four in 1994. "Coach was cool all year. There was no stress," he said. "We were good and we knew it, and he coached us up appropriately. He had us prepared every night."

Reggie Geary (Courtesy Reggie Geary)

One of the reasons for the success—and it was a big reason throughout his career—was the importance of Bobbi, his first wife. She grounded him, the yin to his yang. She'd be the go-between or sounding board for the players. "You know that saying: 'Behind every good man, there is a great woman,'" Geary said. "That was her. She was on par with him. Maybe she made him better or gave him confidence to do what he did. She kept him grounded. She kept him in touch. She knew our girlfriends. She knew when things weren't going well with the girlfriends. And she'd relay it to Coach, telling him 'Maybe go easier on him.' She was great at that, a perfect coach's wife. She was a big part of it. She was part of the family, the show, part of everything. He needed someone as special as him to make all that go smoothly. She did a great job."

Olson's relationship with Geary was also great. He was a three-year captain on some pretty good teams. "He felt a lot for me," Geary said. "He gave me a lot of confidence. He knew I had a high basketball IQ and was intelligent. He liked that. I think he respected me."

There was an instance Geary's freshman year that may have established that respect. "He grabbed my arm to talk to me. He may have grabbed me by my elbow, and I pulled back," Geary said. "And I told him, 'Don't do that.' I don't recall him ever doing it again. He realized don't do that with Reggie. But we always had good relationship, and it was always very respectful. He had that respect, and that's why he hired me not once—but twice."

After nine years of pro ball in the NBA and overseas, Geary returned. "I expressed interest in coming back to coach, and he thought it would be a great idea, and I still had to get my degree," he said. "So, I got my degree, hung around the team a little bit, did some high school coaching at the same time."

The timing was ideal. Rodney Tention left to take a head coaching job, and Geary was placed on the staff. "The first time didn't work out. It wasn't what I had been presented, which was unfortunate because my role changed," he said. "I ended up doing the one year, but it was a great year. He still treated me as a coach. He still gave me a voice in that room where I could be part of the decision-making process. I always respected that."

A couple of years later after coaching in the D League, Geary returned to Arizona again as an assistant. "He was trying to make the situation right," Geary said. "And I appreciated that."

Geary's second coaching stint came at a difficult time. Arizona had just dismissed Kevin O'Neill and brought in Mike Dunlap, Russ Pennell, and Geary. Olson had taken the previous year off during the O'Neill year. "Coach and I spent a lot of time together that year," Geary said of 2008. "I was kind of a confidant. I traveled with him the majority of the year. We went on most recruiting trips. We went to camps. It was a different time in his career."

Geary said he just saw Olson getting older. Times were changing. "Recruiting was still his main focus, though," Geary said.

Then, came the fall of 2008 when it was announced he would step away from the game. He had a stroke, and his health became a factor. "It was a difficult time," Geary said. "We knew something wasn't right [with Coach]. We also knew that's not how we wanted him to go out or he wanted to go out. That was disappointing."

Eventually, Olson recovered and stayed retired, and as most every former player said, the relationship became less player to coach and more player to friend. "It's cool," Geary said. "You enjoy it. Yes, it's a totally different dynamic. You can go and have a wine and beer with him."

Geary still misses his college coach. "We were just talking about him yesterday," he said. "I miss him a lot."

He'll forever be indebted to the man who recruited him and the lessons he learned from him. "What he did that was great was recognize individuals' talents and not trying to fit people into a particular box or system," he said. "He allowed us to do what we do best, whatever that was. Then, he instilled confidence in us to go out and do those things. And he was a great example of how we should conduct ourselves…to be a professional, to be a class act, that you can be all those things and still have fun and be fiercely competitive. And he was very detail-oriented. Yet, he had this real ease about him. He'd mold you a little bit and coach you up without drawing attention to himself or trying to show the world how smart he was."

18

Matt Othick

Sometimes fate finds a way to get you somewhere. It did for Matt Othick, a clean-cut guard from Las Vegas. The perfect scenario would have had him playing for Jerry Tarkanian and UNLV in the late 1980s, early 1990s. But his high school coach, Al La Rocque, who played for Lute Olson at Long Beach City College, had set up some playing time with older players and Othick so Olson could observe. "I was a scrawny little guy at the time. Heck, I was throughout my college career," Othick said. "But I had a really good day playing against the guys. Lute liked how I played. I felt that I could go to Arizona, and he really wanted me to go. It was kind of perfect timing given that Steve Kerr was in his senior year."

The timing was such that UNLV was going to get a point guard from the University of Portland named Greg Anthony. Othick and Anthony had played against one another in high school. Anthony, a Vegas native, was coming back to UNLV to play. Othick said Tarkanian had guaranteed Anthony the starting spot. "People say I didn't want to compete against Greg, but that wasn't the case," Othick said. "He was guaranteed the spot, so it wasn't up for grabs. So it just had me wanting to go to Arizona."

Arizona had always appealed to Othick because of the Wildcats' fast-paced play and style. Kerr was leaving, and Matt

Muehlebach and Kenny Lofton returned. "When you're young you think you're the greatest thing on Earth. It's not like I didn't respect their abilities," Othick said. "I just thought I could fit in well and play there, which ended up happening."

Right away, he was mentioned by media and fans as being the next Kerr. "That was always a tough thing for me because I really played differently than Steve when I came out of high school," he said. "As I matured, Lute molded me into who he wanted me to be, so I did play more like Steve—not that it's not an amazing thing. He was a great player. But I'd say I was, well, a little flashier. Coach wanted a guy who could shoot the ball and wouldn't turn the ball over. I always battled with Coach."

Olson wanted a guard who would take care of the ball. "I remember a scrimmage when I was a freshman where I had 25 points and had 10 assists but had five turnovers in the game," Othick recalled. "All Coach wanted to talk about was my five turnovers. I'll never forget it because it woke me up to realize I've got to play perfect for Arizona. It was just a different style of basketball that I played over my career."

There was some resistance as Othick developed into the kind of player Olson wanted. "I fought it, and Coach and I had a great relationship," he said. "I'd never disrespected him. I respected him so much as a coach and as a person and how he molded us into men. But, yes, I hated it. I didn't want to be Steve Kerr. I wanted to be Matt Othick. So, that was tough for me, really tough for me. I had played a certain way my whole life. I'd never had a coach push back. Obviously, as you rise and you play the higher level, you have coaches who have had great success doing things a certain way."

It took three years for that to finally take hold. "It was my senior year, and I did have a lot of great games," he said. "I had great success at Arizona. There was a time there that I finally figured out exactly what he wanted for me. And in turn he gave me a little more leeway because at the same time he saw who I was. I got what he wanted from me, and it really worked…I didn't love everything he tried to get me to do on a basketball floor. But what I realized as I got older, he turned me into a solid defender. When I got to Arizona, I was so driven by offense. I'd save energy and do everything else because I was kind of a thin kid. He demanded defensive intensity all the time and he turned me into a good defender by my sophomore year. And, offensively, he pushed me. It was tough sometimes. I'm a coach's son. I understand the game. I understood the game at a pretty high level. When I made a mistake, I knew the mistake. Sometimes he'd get on me about it and I already knew what it was, and it was just different for me as a point guard."

Othick fondly remembers a 1990 game against another powerhouse program of that era. "I'll never forget we were playing in Madison Square Garden against Arkansas," he said. "And he walked out on the floor so proud of our team before the game. He turned to me and Matt Muehlebach and said, 'We're really good, guys. We're gonna win this game.' He had never done anything like that. I got chills up and down the spine. We crushed them, and they were [highly ranked]. That was a special moment."

Arizona's special coach always had him prepared. "He demanded respect and he did it by the way he carried himself," Othick said. "I always had great respect for him. He knew the game inside and out. The thing I thought he was best at was how prepared he was. I tell people that all the time. He was the best at it. I mean 98 percent of the games we played in we had already won, and the game hadn't even started. We won before we even hit the floor."

That confidence grew on the players. They embodied their coach with their play. "Absolutely, it was that confidence," Othick said. "He just rubbed off on our teams. We had the 71-game win streak [because of it]. I only had one loss in my career at home. It was a brutal loss but only one loss."

That loss to UCLA shows that nothing is perfect. And neither was Olson. He was demanding. And sometimes he couldn't get his point across. One frustrating early-season trip to Oregon to face Oregon and Oregon State proved that. After beating Michigan in the season opener, UA faced the two teams in

From left to right: Lute Olson,
Matt Othick, and Jerry Tarkanian
(Courtesy Matt Othick)

Oregon, and UA, surprisingly, got swept. In between games at a practice, Olson got so upset with his players that he kicked a ball into the stands. "He was frustrated with all of us," he said. "It was just none of us was playing well...He got us prepared, but we didn't bring it to the floor like he prepared us. He was not very happy, and I'd say I probably had one of my worst couple of games I've ever played in my life. It was a horrible road trip. It was to start the year. The great thing about that was we finished the year with Oregon State the last game of the year and returned the favor and whipped them to win the Pac-10 championship. It was full circle. Coach was so proud of the progress we made."

But it wasn't a great start to the season for Arizona or Othick. After a solid game against Michigan, then the debacle at Oregon, Othick was asked to get the team in better shape both physically and mentally. "He rode me harder than I've ever been ridden in my life for about two weeks," Othick said. "I had never lost my confidence playing basketball. And I lost my confidence after that road trip, and it took me about three weeks to get myself back together.

"He was more concerned about defense. He just wanted effort. And he knew that our team needed to be tougher. Remember: he wasn't used to losing. None of us were. We were all winners. I had never seen him so upset, and still he never said a curse word. He was mad at us for literally two, three weeks. Every practice we dreaded going to. It was tough. But we started to come out of it by Christmas. We got going, turned the corner, and everything was good."

But at the end of the season, Arizona fell to Alabama in the second round of the NCAA Tournament. It came a year after UA lost in heart-breaking fashion to UNLV as the No. 1 team in the nation. And then UA fell to Seton Hall in 1991 in the Sweet 16 and then to East Tennessee State his senior year. All were crushing blows for a group of players who had great careers. "All I cared about was winning one for Coach," he said. "I really wanted to be that guard that could say I helped Coach Olson win a national title. That's what mattered to me more than anything. As I look back on my career, that's what hurts the most."

Othick reflected on his relationship with Olson. "I had a good relationship with Coach—not a great relationship," he said. "I didn't fight with him. There was no fight to have. If you did, you'd lose. You do what he says. That's why he was a great coach and why he had that respect. But the first few years after I left, I would say I just stayed away. It was a tough way to end my career, losing in the first round of the NCAA Tournament. I just went away from Arizona for a few years. I just feel like I let him down, that I let the city down. I was a competitor and didn't like losing and wouldn't accept it. I was young and didn't handle it well. Then maybe eight or 10 years after I was done, I came back and I had a great relationship the rest of his time there."

Coach and player started visiting again. Othick opened a couple of pizza chains in the San Diego, where Olson had a second home nearby. "I'd see him when he'd come to the restaurant," he said. "He was hugely supportive. I'd talk to him often on the phone. We had great conversations. It really sealed the deal in my decision of going to Arizona because here I was 20 to 30 years later talking to my coach, and he was like my father. And that was special to me."

Othick still remembers the lessons he learned from Olson. "The No. 1 thing was discipline. The second thing I learned was how organized he was," he said. "He was the most organized and disciplined guy I'd ever seen. And he was a hell of a competitor. That's where he and I were exactly the same."

And it's the reason they butted heads from time to time. "I was stubborn, but I always respected him," he said. "His involvement in the community—he was great at that. I've learned the importance. He helped people that needed help. We'd go to hospitals to see patients. That part of the Arizona basketball program to me was special."

Othick said he'll miss him and those golf outings in San Diego and those meetings at Del Mar Thoroughbred Club, a place where Othick reunited old rivals Olson and Tarkanian one summer day. "I loved Tark, always did," Othick said. "But they had so much animosity, I guess, for each other for a while. I just would never say anything bad about either one of them. I love both. So, it was a difficult situation."

So, it was more than impressive to get the two to take a picture together while they were both attending a day at the races at Del Mar. "In the later years, they had let a lot of things go," Othick said. "They just happened to be at the track that day and on the same floor. I just said I was going to make the meeting happen. I grabbed them and I said, 'I want to take a picture with you guys.' It turned out to be a great picture."

The two Hall of Fame coaches ended up speaking to one another afterward. "That was super cool," he said. "It was a great moment in my life."

Credit Othick, a point guard, with another assist.

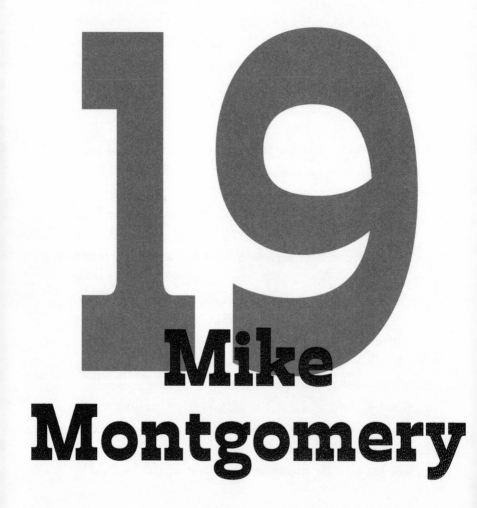

19
Mike Montgomery

Mike Montgomery could have been an assistant coach for Lute Olson many years ago. It was a possibility. Imagine what that would have looked like. In 1973–74 Olson was the coach of Long Beach State, and a young Montgomery was looking to return to his alma mater after the coaching staff at the University of Florida—of which he was a part—had been let go. By then, Montgomery had been an assistant coach at Coast Guard, Citadel, and Colorado State. "I didn't have any luck," Montgomery said. "I had graduated from there and I thought it was logical, but it didn't happen."

Montgomery had marveled at Olson. "The first impression you get when you meet Lute is that he's stately," Montgomery said. "He carries himself and presents himself so well. He's a big man, good looking, and not overly demonstrative. He has a nice smile and a way about him. You think, *This guy could be a senator.*"

Fast forward 12 years, and Olson and Montgomery would meet plenty of times in the then-Pac-10, where the two eventual coaching titans would rule the conference for nearly 25 years. The majority of the time it was either Arizona or Stanford winning the conference title. In the head-to-head battles, Olson-led Arizona went 28–12 against Montgomery-coached teams.

The games, however, were epic. "He had players, just not household-name players," Montgomery said. "I had inherited some players. At the time UCLA and Arizona were at the top of the heap. I asked my guys: 'How many guys here were recruited by UCLA, Arizona, North Carolina, Duke?' No hands went up. So, I told them, 'We have some work to do. How are we going to catch those people?' It was about establishing a work ethic."

Olson and the Wildcats also had a great home-court advantage. "They were impossible to beat in Tucson once he got that crowd going," Montgomery said. "Even though we were pretty good, we were getting beat substantially—a lot. It was a hard place to go and get a win."

Under Montgomery, Stanford was able to beat Arizona in his first two years. One victory occurred in 1988 when Arizona was ranked No. 1 in the country, and Stanford had the likes of Adam Keefe and Todd Lichti. "Obviously, the first group at Stanford was good," Montgomery said. "Then we built it back up with Brevin Knight and others. But winning down there was tough. Our first breakthrough was huge."

Beating Arizona was a big deal. "Lute was always gracious but didn't like it because he hated to lose," Montgomery said. "The Pac-10 at the time was his fiefdom. And you don't want people infringing on the throne. He had it well-established down there."

In contrast to the "stately" Olson, Montgomery jokingly referred to himself as a coach who "runs around and is after the officials not like anyone would pay attention."

Olson had a different style. "When he walked down on the court to the end of the score table and folded his arms and glared at the officials, it was probably more effective than my ranting

Mike Montgomery
(AP Images)

and raving," Montgomery said. "People might think he didn't say much, but he controlled the game. He had the respect. When he was unhappy, he'd let them know it. We had some games that broke his heart and games that broke mine. I think both of us coached the game in a sort of a similar way in that we weren't wild. We weren't going to beat ourselves by just turning the ball over and making bad decisions. I do know we had some great games."

In one of those great games, Khalid Reeves raced the length of the court with five seconds left to beat Stanford 72–70 in 1992. In another, Damon Stoudamire went for 45 points in an 89–83 overtime win in Palo Alto, California. Stanford's Nick Robinson hit a shot from beyond halfcourt to beat UA 80–77 in 2004. Arizona's Michael Wright's last-second shot in front of a crazed Stanford crowd in 2001 took down the Cardinal.

UA beat No. 3 Stanford 78–76 in 1999, and Arizona fans stormed the court. "I remember remarking that the fans were so into it," Montgomery said. "I went to the press room, and said, 'You know, our guys have feelings, too. They're trying to win, too.' I don't remember ever having any contentious situations where anybody was out of control. Lute wouldn't want that. He didn't like that kind of thing; either did I. At the end of the day, it was a game, and they were kids trying to compete."

A true competitor, Montgomery did all he could to make his mark against Olson. "I guess part of my thing was trying to earn his respect as a young coach, coming into the league and with a background of not being a very good player in college, all that kind of stuff, just trying to earn his respect," he said. "Grudgingly, we did that. Eventually, we went to Tucson and beat them a time or two. It wasn't going to be a big loss, but we had a chance to win. It became more of a fun thing for us in terms of a rivalry. Any time you beat Arizona, you knew you had accomplished something."

Montgomery said part of the home-court advantage was because of how the McKale Center crowd impacted the referees. "Lute might turn over in his grave if he heard this, but the officials were intimidated by that crowd," he said. "They saw every call as being wrong when it went against them and they let the officials know that. That's what you try to create in a home court."

The rivalry brought out the best in both teams. "Lute knew they'd have to be prepared to beat us," Montgomery said. "We felt the same. He also had very good players. They always had talent, but he also always took players and made them better."

Montgomery recruited Luke Walton and Matt Muehlebach, among other players, and Arizona recruited some players that eventually ended up at Stanford, including the Collins twins—Jarron and Jason. "It was a fun rivalry," he said.

As for the relationship, well, the two respected one another greatly. "He wasn't a guy that required a lot of people to be around him and pat his back…at least outwardly," Montgomery said. "He kept a pretty close group of people around him. I don't remember him being real outgoing, a talk-to-everyone, arm-around-them-kind-of-guy. But we were friendly with him and Bobbi. Bobbi was very special, a great wonderful gal."

Montgomery went to Bobbi's memorial service in 2001. "They were a formidable couple, for sure," he said. "But it wasn't one of those deals where you could call Lute and say, 'Let's have dinner. Hey, let's go have a drink.' But as time went on, when we did Nike trips, we'd always end up playing golf together and we'd end up sitting and having dinner together."

Who was the better golfer? "Oh, come on, you know who was...I was younger," said Montgomery, who joked that Olson's long stays in the NCAA Tournament prevented him from working on his game. "Plus, he was deep into the postseason, and I wasn't...My nature is to needle people, and I mostly did it on the golf course with him. He was older. He had a good short game, could get up and down and chip and putt with the best of them. But my thing was to needle him. He'd look at me in that dignified way. He was never one to get down and dirty. He was always a gentleman. He'd just shake his head and give one of his looks and kind of chuckle."

Montgomery greatly admired what Olson did on the court at Arizona. "That place wasn't always a national championship-type contender place," he said. "He sort of turned it into that just based on good kids working hard, getting guys to play well together, and most of them stayed four years."

After Olson retired, Montgomery reached out a number of times just to say hello, see how he was doing, and reminisce. "I just felt like it was important," Montgomery said. "We'd gone back a long way. I don't know what he was dealing with. I just felt like it was important that, at least to me, to make sure he knew I was thinking about him and for him to know how important he was in my life and how much I treasured our competition in our time together."

20
Jawann McClellan

Jawann McClellan had a unique bond with Lute Olson for his entire career and beyond. Some players don't get to experience that closeness, that back-and-forth McClellan had with Coach Olson. He first met Olson at Walt Disney World in Florida during a summer league tournament. He was 15, about to turn 16 years old. "I always had a relationship with Josh Pastner since I was probably like seven or eight years old. Josh has already seen me play," McClellan said. "But I saw Coach on the sideline at the event. Then, the next thing you know, I saw him again, then again, and then again. Then word got back to me that he was very interested in me."

It was after Olson's third appearance at a game that McClellan realized Olson was interested in him. And that was perfect given McClellan had always pegged Arizona as his dream school. After Olson's sixth visit to a game, McClellan was offered a scholarship. "When I made a basket, we made eye contact," he said. "He kind of smiled with his smile. And that was a way of, I guess, him telling me that he was impressed."

McClellan was hooked. How could he not be? One problem: McClellan was in the process of committing to Marquette and Tom Crean. "People didn't know that about Marquette," McClellan said. "So, I had to call Coach Crean and tell him I was no longer interested. I committed to Arizona two days later. I regret doing it like that, but at the time, this is what it was because I knew where I wanted to go."

The University of Texas had also been in the picture. "It tried to come in after I had already been committed [to Arizona]."

And, well, Olson had already made his impression given he was the builder of the Arizona basketball program and was in one of McClellan's impressionable movies, *He Got Game*. "He had a presence because you gotta remember he was in that movie," McClellan said. "It had come out a little before the recruitment. He said in the movie that, 'This is one of the most important decisions in your life.'"

Another draw, of course, was that Olson was a coaching luminary. "At the time he might not have been known as the best coach of all time, but he had that Dean Smith, John Thompson feel about him," McClellan said. "People say when they first meet Michael Jordan and they get speechless. Well, Coach O had that about him. Then you get to Tucson and you understand why."

When he got to Tucson, McClellan was treated like a pro. "It was kind of like a business," McClellan said. "I'm not sure that was typical. He didn't treat us like we were 18- and 19-year-old kids. He pretty much treated us like we were pros, adults. That's why we didn't have curfews and stuff like that. You're here to be a pro and not here to be a jack-around. If you are going to be, you won't be here anymore. That was always his mind-set."

And then a bond was forged. "I still can't believe that I had the relationship with Coach Olson because I still look at him as *this* guy," McClellan said. "It's hard for me to even say the word 'Lute.' I'm 36 years old now. I still think of him as my coach. I'm

Jawann McClellan on
Senior Day in 2008 (AP Images)

sure a lot of people had that persona about him and were able to call him Lute. Hey, don't get me wrong, I definitely had my issues with him where maybe I had to sit in the locker room after the USC, UCLA weekend when [we] hadn't played well. He just came over to us and asked what was wrong. He just said, he didn't think we had a practice to be proud of or where he didn't think I was worthy of playing. We moved on from there."

McClellan wasn't intimidated by Olson. Instead he saw him as more of a father figure. "That happened because of my personality," he said. "A lot had to do with my daddy. And I think a lot of people or players would just be scared of a coach to be honest, but that wasn't me. I didn't care about being in fear of not playing in the game because my mind-set was like, *I'm good enough.*"

McClellan felt comfortable poking fun of his coach. "I would always put bunny ears behind his head or hit him on the back or hit him on the butt," he said. "There was a time I ran him over in practice [in a drill accidentally]. He got a good laugh. I just wanted him to stay loose because I saw the business side of him. He was always business."

McClellan chalked that playfulness up to being a naïve freshman. "I really didn't understand. I was just having fun, to be honest. I had no clue as to what was going on," he said. "And I think that's what helped me in our relationship."

That relationship changed the summer before his sophomore year when McClellan's father had a heart attack while driving and died in a one-car crash. It was June of 2005. At the time Olson was on a family vacation in Italy. "He showed me his true colors," McClellan said. "He flew back to see me for one day."

Olson attended the funeral. McClellan said it's something he will always remember. "He told me, 'I don't care if you come back [to UA]. If you want to leave to go get closer to your family and be with your mom and you want to go to [University of Texas], I will grant it.' He said, 'I will make sure to do everything in my power to make sure you have eligibility right away.' He's telling me this. He's telling one of the guys who potentially could be one his star players the next year. He was willing to do that... that showed me a lot about his character."

McClellan was ready to transfer. All he had to do was take care of business in Houston, get back to Tucson to get his stuff, and then get to Texas. "I had nothing else to think about, just what I needed to do for school," he said.

But then he thought of his dad. "My daddy would always tell me: 'A man is judged by his word,' and I gave Coach Olson my word," McClellan said. "He did nothing for me to leave. It was just a tragic accident that he had nothing to do with, no control. For this man to fly from Italy and spend some time with me... that's all I needed to know...I was very fortunate to have my dad and to have Coach O."

McClellan remembered the time at the first practice in his UA career when it was so brutal. It was unfathomably tough, especially for the first one of the year. "You were going against All-Americans. Hell, all of them were. I was one," he said. "I got a sprained toe, so I subbed myself out. It was really bad...I never got back in. I called my dad, and said, 'I'm not sure this place is for me.' And he said, 'You have one option: either you can stay and figure it out because you can't come back home.'"

His dad wanted him to stay with Coach Olson. "Coach O always had my dad's support," he said.

In fact, McClellan said one of the big reasons he got along so well with Olson was because he saw a lot of the same qualities in them. "Coach Olson was kind of like the White version of him," he said. "My dad was Black, and that was the only difference between them. He hammered me when I would be a [knucklehead], when I needed to get in line."

McClellan thought of Coach Olson like a second dad. "It feels funny saying that because he's White," he said, laughing. "But a lot of us looked at him like that, still do to this day. He was there for me. He was there for Steve Kerr…He was there for a lot of key players."

After McClellan's father had been gone for a few years, Coach Olson started going through his own health issues, sitting out that 2008 season because of a stroke. No one had been in contact with Olson the entire year…well, except for McClellan. "He was a reason why I was at Arizona, and I wanted him there for the Senior Day," McClellan said. "He's one of the reasons I even had a Senior Day. One day I saw him in the weight room and I broke down to him and I said, 'Coach, I know that you don't feel good, but I'm asking you if you can just come out to my Senior Day.'"

So Olson came out to honor his senior and give him a big hug. The crowd roared. "He surprised everybody," McClellan said. "I broke down crying because there was a lot of emotion buildup because I didn't think he was going to come. He wasn't feeling good. People don't even know how he got there, and I'm not taking credit for him going there. But we had a conversation, and he was there. People think that I cried because of my dad [not being there], and that had something to do with it, but that wasn't everything. Lute showed up."

Through the tears, all McClellan remembered was "he grabbed me and wouldn't let me go. We didn't have a conversation." There was one later, however, as Olson told him he had to get his degree no matter what.

McClellan came back and finished that degree in 2009. He's now a police officer in Houston, his hometown. He tried his hand at coaching, but by that time, Olson was out of coaching, and McClellan figured real life was calling. "Everything happened for a reason," he said. "When I was a young man, I was still trying to figure out what I was going to do. Now I have three kids and am married. It's just different now. I have a son now. Maybe his career will be better than mine. You never know."

He'll tell his sons and his daughters, who are also very good athletes, what Olson told him: "'Worry about your business and handle yourself,'" McClellan said. "Sometimes people would make excuses. He didn't want that. It was: 'Do your job. Don't worry about nobody else.' So, every time my wife says something or my daughter says something, I'm always saying, 'Don't worry about nobody else. Do what she was supposed to do.' I think that's one of the things that stuck with me throughout my adulthood. Do what you are supposed to do, and everything will fall into place."

21
Jason Gardner

C redit Damon Stoudamire for helping Arizona recruit fellow guard Jason Gardner, though he didn't do so directly. Already a big-time program by the late 1990s, Arizona was part of the SEGA Genesis video game, and Gardner's brother used to play Stoudamire in it. "I got to see him play Damon and I started to idolize Damon," Gardner said. "I'd think, *Hey, this little dude is good*...I didn't know anything about Arizona except that. Back then you couldn't really see Arizona play that much [in Indianapolis]. I'd only see them play maybe two or three times a year."

Gardner never met Stoudamire while he was in school from 1991 to 1995 but did meet him one day when he came back for a visit. "We played a little one-on-one, and that was our first meeting," he said. "Talk about an experience. You're talking about people saying he was one of the hardest dudes to guard in the league. He had the three-pointer, he had the pull-up jumper, he had the floater."

Perhaps thinking he had the next Stoudamire, Lute Olson started recruiting Gardner. The talented point guard described their interaction. "I pretty much enjoyed our conversations. He was laid-back and always calm and cool," Gardner said. "He always wanted to know about my family and me. He always had that presence. It was just good talking to him because he was always talking about the right stuff."

When he was recruiting Gardner, Olson always had a presence. "He'd walk in and be wearing that A on his chest. He stood out," he said. "And that hair of his was always on point. It was kind of who he was. You knew when he walked into a room. You knew that was Lute Olson."

Gardner committed, and Olson's impressive track record was a definite selling point. "He told me his history with the guards here, his win percentage, the success of his players, and—whether they go to the pros or not—how successful they are after college in whatever they do," he said. "There was really no gray area. For me, he just said, 'This is what I want you to do, and if you can get better at that, you can do this.' He painted a picture that was clear cut that if he brought you aboard, these were the expectations."

It didn't hurt that Luke Walton and Richard Jefferson were his host recruits. "Luke is a little more reserved, and Richard is a bit more different, laughing and has a big personality," he said. "It was a great combination and fit. And it's a reason why they got along so well."

And, indeed, Gardner fit in well. He was the guard who started right away. In fact, he started all but one game in his career while helping lead Gilbert Arenas, Jefferson, Michael Wright, and Loren Woods. Walton and Ricky Anderson were on the bench. Was there pressure leading such a talented group? "No, not at all, he didn't do that," he said. "But when you go to Arizona, there is some pressure whether you're a starter or you redshirt or you play [whatever] number of minutes. If you come to Arizona, you have to expect pressure because there is going to be some. At some point you want to be that guy where you walk on the court and you want that to be on you."

Gardner welcomed that attention. "Mike Bibby had left, Jason Terry had left, so I came in with big expectations where I wanted to be a star at Arizona," he said. "Lute never really talked to me about it. I just had my own expectations about being at Arizona and what I wanted...Coach wasn't a talker, although you did have some conversations. He's bringing you in because he saw something in you. He knows you can play the game or saw something athletically. Maybe you'd have a couple of bad practices or a couple of bad games. That's when he'd sit you down and talk. We'd talk about what's going on. But he never put pressure on me because he knew I put enough pressure on myself that he didn't have to add pressure."

Even as a freshman, Gardner became a leader. "Coach did a lot of things early on," he said, "but as time went on and the team continued to get better, he thought *This little freshman gets it.* I remember Loren pulling me aside at halftime of a game and told me, 'Hey, just run the show. We're going to listen to you.' Coming from Loren, who was one of the leaders of the team, that meant a lot. I took off from there. I think Coach O realized I was trying to get the guys in the right position and think the game."

It wasn't always a good thing. Back in 2003, when Arizona was one of the top teams in the country, Olson had seen enough of his team to know it wasn't listening to him or the other coaches. They had barely defeated Washington [88–85 in overtime], so he decided to let his captains coach practice

Jason Gardner
(AP Images)

before the Washington State game in Pullman, Washington. It was an eye-opener to his players. UA eventually got the sweep. "He was a great relationship guy," Gardner said. "He trusted his team to do different things. He was a player's coach. He'd break things down for you and give you what you needed, but he also let us go out and play."

Gardner recalled Olson leaving for two to three weeks while grieving the loss of his wife, Bobbi. Arizona was still one of the best teams in the country despite dealing with the absence of Olson. Assistant coach Jim Rosborough replaced him, and Arizona went 3–1 during that juncture. "As young men you worry about him, but Coach Roz did a great job holding down the fort," he said. "But it had to be tough on him. He had a great relationship with Bobbi. You could tell they loved one another. When I'd be out of sorts and Lute wasn't unavailable, I'd talk to Bobbi, and she'd make me feel comfortable, assuring me that it was a family atmosphere. Losing her was tough. They'd been together for more than 40-something years. There's a lot of history for someone to be by his side. He didn't really show his emotions, but you could feel it. He was always trying to show strength to the players that, *Yes, I'm going through something, but we're going to get through this together.*"

Then came the run to the championship game in 2001 vs. No. 1 Duke. Arizona was No. 2. The highest-ranked teams going into the season appropriately faced each other in the finals. "It was a great run," he said. "We all came here to play for Coach Olson. It was a great game. We all had great friendships and gained brothers along the way. We fought for one another. We had a shot, but they got hot there in the second half late in the game. We had ultra-competitive guys in the locker room. So a lot of guys were upset and sad that we lost."

One moment caught in the postgame locker room was Olson going to Arenas, Wright, Woods, and Jefferson and thanking them for playing for Arizona and making the year special. Arenas, Wright, and Jefferson were going to declare for the NBA. Woods was in his senior year. "It was the next chapter of their lives," said Gardner, who also declared but ended up coming back.

But Arizona basketball never stops. New players came in, and Olson coached them up. He had guys like Hassan Adams, Andre Iguodala, Channing Frye, and Salim Stoudamire join the likes of Walton and Gardner. In 2003 Arizona was again ranked No. 1 from the beginning of the season, holding that spot for 13 weeks. No team in Olson's time had been ranked No. 1 in a season longer than that team. "It was another great year. We thought we'd go to the national title game again and play Syracuse," he said. "We had a lot of shooters and some big rebounders. We had Ricky Anderson, a shooter, and we had Andre and Luke working the middle with Channing. We had a lot of good players."

It came down to Arizona and Kansas. And this time, unlike 1997, Kansas prevailed 78–75. Gardner took the last shot for a tie. After all, he had been given the nickname Mr. Big Shot after hitting big shots throughout his career. "Coach gave me the freedom for those shots," he said. "As a kid when you're playing in the driveway, you dream of those moments. I was that guy who was comfortable taking those shots or I was the guy who wanted the ball in my hand because I loved those situations good or bad."

Olson gave him that latitude. "He trusted me and my decision-making under pressure," he said. "That whatever the defense the opponent had, I'd get through it and make the right read."

Nearly 20 years later—and one year after Olson's passing—Gardner was brought back by new coach Tommy Lloyd to be on his coaching staff. It had come full circle for the former All-American, something Olson would've appreciated. "He'd be loving it," Gardner said. "He'd be excited and happy that I was back."

Like all the others, he misses him. "He's why I came to Arizona," he said. "I had a great time here and loved the community. I have always loved this place."

And the community loved him right back. He finished with the third most points in school history (1,984) and fifth most in a season (692). He also had the second most three-pointers (318) and ranks first in minutes played (4,825). But Gardner credits Olson and the other players around him. "I had a great coaching staff leading me and I had some very talented teammates," he said. "It was because of my great relationship with Coach Olson. He always knew I wanted to be on the court. He knew I was feisty and competitive. He knew I wanted to win every game."

22

Paul Weitman

If there was an insider to Robert Luther Olson, it was Paul Weitman, a local businessman and Olson's longtime friend. In fact, some might have considered them brothers, considering the time they spent together and that they were both tall, regal men who loved the game of basketball. One was a successful businessman; the other was a successful college basketball coach. And, well, they were constant companions during basketball season and away from it. Oftentimes—perhaps more times than you can count—Lute, Bobbi, Paul, and Betty (Paul's late wife) were at each other's houses for dinners or get-togethers. "He loved an occasional glass of wine, and so did I," Weitman said. "Our wives did, too. We'd cook on the grill. He loved my Georgia ribs."

It's how it started back in the mid-1980s when Lute Olson first arrived in Tucson in 1983. It was like that for nearly 20 years before Bobbi's passing in 2001 and before Lute's passing in 2020. No one spent more time with Olson at Arizona road games than Weitman, and surely no one walked more miles with Olson than Weitman. There were hundreds, perhaps thousands of miles walked during those early mornings before big games and those off days between games. "He sure liked to walk a lot," Weitman said. "It was his way of staying fit. I enjoyed it, too.

We'd talk about a lot of different things…family, players, teams, basketball."

One early morning while on an away game, the two went walking as did the team. Many times, the players didn't like getting up early to take that walk, but they did it. "He didn't want them sleeping late before an early-morning game," Weitman said, telling the story at Olson's celebration of life in the fall of 2021. "Needless to say, most of these young guys, especially the freshmen, would rather have stayed in bed. Lute had a saying: 'The best thing about freshmen is they become sophomores.' One morning when we were in California, I remember Lute and I were walking behind the team. It was a slow pace—one set by the players—when I noticed one player jump into the bushes and hide. When we circled back to finish the walk, the player jumped out of the bushes and right back into pack without being noticed. I saw it all. But I never told Lute. Since I know the player is listening now, I want to say sorry to Lute for not telling him. And to the sly player who jumped into the bushes—and who just might be in this room—your secret is still safe with me."

Weitman proved to be loyal to everyone. But he was closest and most loyal to Olson. In fact, before Olson became the head coach in the spring of 1983—after a successful run at Iowa —Weitman took a liking to Olson. Being that he was also a successful former high school coach, Weitman noticed—and followed—good college coaches. How could one not notice Olson? He was successful at Long Beach State, then at Iowa. And Weitman thought if Arizona ever needed a coach, it should be Olson.

Even before Dave Strack hired Ben Lindsey from Grand Canyon College, Weitman thought Olson would be a great fit. Instead, Strack hired Lindsey, who proceeded to drive the program into the college basketball ditch. By then Cedric Dempsey was the new athletic director at Arizona. Dempsey and Weitman became fast friends, too, and oftentimes Dempsey would ask Weitman who he thought would be good for UA.

Olson's name always came up. "I followed Lute closely. He had a great record and he had just taken Iowa to the Final Four,"

Paul Weitman at Bobbi Olson's memorial service (AP Images)

Weitman said. "He had been a high school coach, he coached at Long Beach City College, Long Beach State, and his record was great at those places. Then I saw that he was good at recruiting good people. There are a lot of people who live in Tucson from Iowa, and I'd run into them, and I'd say, 'You have a good basketball coach,' and they'd say, 'Oh, man, oh, yeah, we do!' So, I watched him more, watching him on TV. I liked the way he looked and how he handled himself. I liked the style he played, and he had guys like Ronnie Lester. He was a great recruiter."

After firing Lindsey, Dempsey famously went to Kansas City, Missouri, during the 1983 NCAA Tournament to possibly talk to Olson just in case Iowa lost. As it turned out, Iowa did, falling to Villanova. The next day, the Olsons met with Dempsey and he convinced Lute and Bobbi to visit Tucson. "All of a sudden," Weitman said, "Cedric calls to tell me he has a coach coming in and he wanted me to talk to him. I said, 'Who is it?' And he said, 'Who did you want?' Heck, I couldn't remember who I told him. I had given him three names."

Dempsey interjected when Weitman couldn't remember. "What a minute," Dempsey told Weitman. "Who did you want?"

"You mean Lute Olson?" Weitman said.

Of course, Weitman met with the Olsons once they got into town. His first impression? "How could you not like him?" Weitman said. "My first impression was very good, but the total package was he had Bobbi. It was even better than I thought."

Weitman was there when Lute and Bobbi said yes to the Arizona job. "Cedric was happy, and I was so happy," Weitman said. "I'm thinking, *Shit this is good*. I call my wife to get some things ready because I wanted to celebrate, have Cedric and

June [Cedric's wife] over to the house to have champagne or something."

In discussions with Olson many years later, Weitman said Olson told him he probably never would have come to Arizona (when UA eventually hired Lindsey) given that he was in the middle of a fund-raising project for the new Hawkeye Arena and just on the heels of a Final Four appearance in 1980. "I was always struck by how much Lute was driven to success both in his coaching and his personal life," Weitman said at his celebration of life. "He spoke about his players fondly but drove them hard on and off the court to be the best they could be. He wanted success for them. He wanted his players to seek excellence not just in their sport but in their lives. He wanted that for every member of his team—the trainers, managers, assistant coaches—everyone."

Given all the success they all seemingly have had, it showed. But when it came to the walks and talking all things basketball and Arizona, the conversations were mostly one-sided. "No, he never asked for my advice, but I gave it to him, of course," said Weitman, a former high school coach in Atlanta. "Sometimes he'd agree and sometimes he wouldn't."

But if there was someone Olson trusted, it was Weitman. And that was something special given Olson loved his privacy when it came to his personal life, even though he was perhaps the biggest public figure in southern Arizona and arguably the entire state. "Everyone knew him," Weitman said. "We'd be somewhere, and someone would recognize him."

That was especially the case in a basketball setting. "We're in San Antonio at the Final Four and we're walking around the Alamodome," Weitman said. "I told him it felt like he was stalking the darn thing because he wanted to get back there for a Final Four—when we finally got done walking, we got on an escalator to get back to the hotel, and someone yells, 'Hey, Lute, how you doing?' He couldn't avoid it."

Sometimes he had better luck getting away from it all in Tuscson. "He told me he'd be out on the lake [in Iowa] and on a boat, and people would find out he's out there and they'd come by and pull up next to him and say, 'Hi, Lute,'" Weitman said. "We'd be in Europe, and people would come up and say, 'Hi, Lute.' He'd be in restaurants with Bobbi eating a nice meal, and people would come up to him while he was eating and say, 'Sorry to bother you, but I wanted to say hello.' It didn't happen here [Tucson] that much."

Paul and Betty were there for perhaps the most harrowing time in the Olson's life. They had gone to France for a basketball clinic, eventually taking an extended vacation to Prague and Budapest. That's when Bobbi got ill, very ill. "He was scared shitless," Weitman said. "How could someone not be? I was scared."

Bobbi hadn't been feeling well, and after Weitman interviewed a couple of doctors to see her at the hotel per Lute's request, it was determined she was sicker than everyone could imagine. The doctor wanted to take her to the hospital. Emergency surgery was needed. No one knew what the diagnosis was. "I was waiting outside the operating room with Lute for over four hours," Weitman said. "We both felt so scared and helpless."

No one really knew what was going on, but a cyst ended up being removed during surgery, and Weitman went the next day to the United States Embassy to see if he could get help. The doctors eventually told Lute that it was cancer. "You could see the blood drain from his face," Weitman said.

Weitman got on the phone and called the University of Arizona College of Medicine and told them what was going on. One of the doctors told him, "'What that guy has done for this university, I'll have two doctors there in 24 hours.' And they were there," Weitman said. "That's when I left."

They then took her to Germany. They stayed there, got her settled, and operated on her when she was able to get back to Tucson. "He loved her, and she loved him," Weitman said. "He knew that she helped him in life."

Eventually, she was deemed healthy—until she relapsed in late 1999. And she eventually passed away on January 1, 2001. "He had been so stressed out, and I invited him to come to the house to work out so he could release some stress," Weitman said before her passing. "No sooner had he gotten there that they called him to say she wasn't doing well. And he had been there by his side all this time. I remember he was on the treadmill when he got the call. He left right away."

She died not long after.

Weitman misses both of the Olsons, and he credits Lute for building Arizona into a basketball powerhouse. "What impressed me was how quick he took our program from zero to a national championship," Weitman said. "That was special. And he was a friend. That's what he was to Betty and me. Sure, I miss him. We did a lot of things together. He might have had a relationship with somebody else I don't know about, but I was pretty close to him."

23
Ben
Davis

There are players who go to the University of Arizona and arrive in Tucson knowing they have found a home for life—even if they don't end up living there after school is over. Ben Davis found that at UA and Tucson. Lute Olson found him at a junior college in Kansas after stops at the University of Kansas and the University of Florida. Of course, basketball brought them together. "He was so understanding of everybody's situation individually," Davis said. "He was always careful not to treat us all the same. It was like he respected us because of where we came from and who raised you. That was special to me because I had never been to a place like that."

Davis was different. He got to Olson. Some couldn't. Some did, and Davis certainly was one of those. "You could have a lot of talks with Coach Olson, maybe unintentionally a lot of the times because he'd ask you questions and then catch you off guard," Davis said. "You wouldn't think he'd be thinking this or that."

And unlike many other former players, Davis said he went into Olson's office daily. "He'd call me in and ask me how I'm doing, especially my first year," Davis said. "I remember I had my problems with the NCAA and had to sit out the last couple of games and NCAA Tournament [in 1995]. He kept telling me the kind of year I was going to have the next year and how the next year was gonna be exactly the way I wanted it to be, that if I stuck it out, I was gonna see that everything was gonna work out. And it did. I had a great year, and everything worked out exactly how I wanted it and how he said. I was never gonna leave, but the fact that he thought that highly of me boosted me for the next year."

Davis worked hard in the offseason to get ready. Davis came back for his senior year and was a huge reason why Arizona made it to the Sweet 16. "He was the best at building your confidence indirectly," he said. "I say 'indirectly' because he wasn't someone who patted you on the back and stroked you. He did it in a different way. He'd say things to you to let you know you've been working to make the situation change. He expected you to want the situation to change."

Davis, admittedly, had a different relationship with his coach since Olson was more like the CEO of the company, and rarely did players go to see him. "You have to remember that Jessie Evans recruited me out of high school, and by that time, I was three years removed from high school when I came to Arizona," he said. "Coach Johnson couldn't go to see me [because of the rules at the time]. So it was Coach O who went to Hutchinson [Community College]. And, I had been through some stuff. And the past was the past with Coach O. Some of the stuff never came up. He even told me: 'I don't want to know because it's the past.' That's how he was with me. And nothing really happened. I was a kid and made decisions that I wouldn't make now. He never made me feel I had a black cloud hanging over me, or that everyone was out there watching me. He never, ever did that."

In hindsight, Davis said he regretted not going to Arizona out of high school before he ended up attending three different schools. It was Olson who recruited him out of New York City after his AAU team spent the summer in the west playing the basketball circuit. "Everywhere I went," he said, "Coach Olson was there."

But he first went to Kansas, stayed a year, was disappointed he wasn't starting, and then left for Florida for a semester but left there as well after realizing he and then-coach Lon Kruger didn't get along, according to Davis. "He's a great coach obviously but not the same as Lute or Roy Williams—completely different kind of guys," he said. "Coach Olson and Coach Williams recruited pros, and Kruger was used to recruiting guys who were under recruited. I just feel I should not have gone there. I can't explain it. We just didn't get along."

So, he left to attend Hutchinson before he went to Arizona. "The first day I got to Hutch and unpacked my bags, Phil Johnson was the first person to call me," he said. "The second was Mark Gottfried."

Six Pac-10 schools called because he told everyone he was going to play out west. "I told Coach Johnson the first day [that] I was going to Arizona," he said. "I couldn't go anywhere else but to Arizona or someplace like Arizona. I knew the kind of coach Lute Olson was. I already loved him. I had to go there. I knew he had a great reputation. Let me say this: I love Roy Williams. If I had a chance to take back my decision, I would have gone there. But I can't take it back. He said I'd be able to come back, but they said Raef Lafrentz was coming and that I'd be going to the NBA...But Coach Olson was the best one by far, not even close. You learn so many things by just watching him. He did everything the right way all the time. All the dudes at that level do it that way."

Davis felt so deeply for Olson that he spoke at length while honoring him at an event during Olson's later years. Players were given only three minutes to speak, but Davis went for 12 minutes. "He did so much for me," he said. "When I came to Arizona, I needed credibility and I needed someone with credibility to believe in me. I knew I wasn't crazy, but everyone else thought so. From the day I got there, I didn't have to do anything extra for it. I just had to be myself. No one was looking over my shoulder every day. Nobody's checking my classes, and that meant a lot."

At Arizona they treated the players like adults, something Davis appreciated. "That's just how it was," he said. "I tell everybody that. We were student-athletes, and he was like a father figure. We had our father figure, but he's also going to let you be you. He's going to let you grow. Yes, sometimes you're going to go outside the line, but he's going to let you know. At the same time, he's always going to let you grow. And we all respected that. When you're there, you don't see it, but…you have so many more freedoms than other places in the country."

On a trip to Tempe, Arizona, to face Arizona State—a game in which Arizona lost—Davis went out with Chris Oldham, a friend on the Arizona Cardinals. UA stayed overnight in Tempe with plans to fly to Rhode Island the next day out of Phoenix. But Davis missed the bus to go to practice. He, however, was able to get to the hotel and change into his practice gear and take a taxi to practice. The traffic was so bad that he got there at the same time as the team bus did. He thought he made it unnoticed. "I got on the ramp with the team like I was supposed to," he said, laughing. "You know how he yelled at everyone? He did that with me, saying I'd never start another game the rest of the year."

No explanations. No excuses. Olson wanted no part of it. "When we got to Rhode Island, he called me to his room and told me how disappointed he was in me," he said. "He said he knows people like to go out in Tempe, but that I had to make better decisions than that. He said he knows I wanted to start every game, but because I did that, I gave up that right. He didn't want me pouting, and that was it."

He didn't start again until he was a senior.

Having not grown up with a father, Davis found that kind of person in Olson. "My coach at Oak Hill was," he said. "But Coach O was like that, too. I got really close to my high school coach because I went there when I was 13…But whenever you have a good coach and he's doing his job, you're going to feel that he has some father figure qualities too. Coach Olson was great. I went to those other schools, but it feels like I went to Arizona the entire time."

In fact, Davis said that Olson and Arizona kind of saved him. "At the time, everything fell into place when I got to junior college," he said. "When I got to juco, all I had to do was ride the bus. Arizona called first and offered first. They talked about wanting me, that they wanted me out of high school, and that they weren't concerned about what happened in the past. I knew I'd be on a great team and get exposure. I think he knew that I was ready for Arizona. But he also told me that I'd have to work hard to find that success."

Davis said he'll always cherish the times together when he'd visit Tucson after his playing days. Olson would ask about his brother and mother and was concerned about how his former player was doing in life. "If I hadn't gone to Tucson," Davis said, "things wouldn't have worked out for me."

He admitted it was a winding road to get to Tucson. "You never know you're in the wrong place," he said, "until you get to the right place."

And because of Olson, he found the right one.

24
Jack Murphy

There are players, coaches, and students who bleed red and blue. Jack Murphy was all those and more at Arizona and continues to be. His journey to Arizona was perhaps more happenstance than any other student associated with the program. And he's still at Arizona as an assistant coach under Tommy Lloyd. Murphy had worked for Lute Olson in his early days as a former manager, recruiting coordinator, administrative assistant, and director of operations.

The road to Tucson was amazing. And it came through Las Vegas. His high school coach, Al La Rocque, played for Olson at Long Beach City College. That name plays a significant role in Murphy's life. Murphy met Olson on an airplane the summer before his freshman year of high school. He and his sister were flying home from a summer camp, and Olson happened to be sitting in a window seat. Murphy was in the middle seat. "I knew who he was because I was the biggest UNLV fan and I didn't like him," Murphy said, smiling. "I wanted to hate him."

But here was this 14-year-old kid sitting next to one of college basketball's best coaches ever and he found out "he was so nice." "He was literally going through his phone records, writing down recruiting calls that he had made," Murphy said. "He started talking to me, asked me where I was from, how old I was. He told me his former player was the coach at Durango High. It was Al La Rocque."

Murphy failed to make his high school team's freshman team or his sophomore team. A teacher at Durango High encouraged him to become a manager on the varsity team, so he did it. Coach La Rocque "became a second father to me and the rest is history."

In the small world that it is, Murphy's mom worked at the Tropicana hotel and used to get Olson rooms when he was in Las Vegas to recruit. By then, Olson and Murphy had become reacquainted through Coach La Rocque. Still, Arizona wasn't in his future. Murphy was headed to the Air Force Academy. But after two months, Murphy was medically disqualified and sent home. "Coach Olson told coach La Rocque they would take me as a manager. They had just won the national championship in 1997," Murphy said. "They took me in."

So, this kid who loved UNLV—Arizona's hated rival back in the late 1980s to early 1990s—was now a Wildcat. "I loved Tark, and there was that 'Midnight Lute' thing and that UNLV–Arizona rivalry," Murphy said. "One of my greatest childhood memories was Anderson Hunt hitting that shot over Kenny Lofton [in the 1989 Sweet 16 in 1989]."

The switch from UNLV to Arizona wasn't lost on Mark Warkentien, who was the former vice president of operations for the Denver Nuggets when Murphy was with the Nuggets. Warkentien was a former assistant coach at UNLV under Tarkanian. "He used to call me the chameleon," Murphy said. "He said in front of most guys I'm a Wildcat, but in front of Vegas guys, I'm a Rebel. He's not completely wrong because I

Jack Murphy (AP Images)

have that Vegas blood in me. But I love and adore Coach Olson. He meant more to me in my life than almost everyone."

Murphy's start at Arizona was unlike most managers under Olson. Typically, they'd go through interviews with assistant coach Jim Rosborough and then be vetted. There was a process.

But Murphy was all but handpicked by Olson. "My relationship with Coach O was different," he said. "Even when I was a freshman, I was comfortable around him. A lot of the [other managers] were scared and nervous whenever Coach came around, or when he'd talk to them, they would clam up and get nervous. I never did that with Coach O because I knew him differently. I knew him from high school. He'd come around, and I'd see him because of Coach La Rocque. To me, he made me feel like I was part of the family. That probably got me in trouble at times because I was probably too much at ease with Coach O. But he always treated me like a son. He was fantastic to me."

His rapport with Olson was very apparent—or noticeable—to the other managers. "They thought I was a little crazy how I would talk around Coach or what I'd say to Coach," he said. "I'd joke with him. I'd give him a hard time at times. They couldn't believe I would do that."

One day they were walking an airport, and a woman came up to the two of them. "She said, 'Oh, my gosh, you are so handsome. You're even more handsome in person than on TV,'" Murphy recalled. "Coach says, 'Thank you so much. That's so kind.' I said, 'Coach, I'm pretty sure she was talking to me.'"

That's the type of relationship they had. Quips and one-liners. "Other guys were probably not comfortable doing that," he said.

He was very aware of Olson's dry sense of humor and his love for giving Coach Rosborough grief. He was also aware of Olson's penchant for thinking he knew more on subjects he had no idea about. "Coach knew how to fly an airplane, even though he'd never taken a lesson," Murphy said. "He'd have you convinced that he could land the jet, even though he's never been in a cockpit. He just had that aura about him."

He recalled one trip to the Bay Area, and the team bus' lights were not working. And it was getting dark. "The bus driver didn't want to go on the freeway because the headlights," Murphy said. "Coach Olson started to tell the driver which turns to take through Berkeley to get to the hotel. All of us looked around and to each other thinking, *Coach O has no idea where he's going.* But in Coach's mind, he knew exactly where he was going. We eventually got there."

There was that funny side, and then there was that serious side. One of the toughest times of Olson's career, life, and beyond came in the 2000–01 season when his beloved wife, Bobbi, got sick. Olson would eventually be away from his team. It started during the UA's Fiesta Bowl Classic, an event UA had never lost. The Wildcats had gone 41–0 in the Classic, heading into late 2000. "He had sheltered us from what was going on with Mrs. O," Murphy said. "He'd be with her a lot. He never missed practice, but he'd be with her right after. Once practice was over, he'd be gone. We didn't know this at the time, but she was in the hospital, and he'd go be with her. We eventually lost that game to Mississippi State after never losing. We like to call it 41 and Roz [who had taken over the team]."

Murphy recalled Olson going to practice on New Year's Day to inform the team Bobbi passed away. She had passed that same day. "I don't think we ended up practicing, but he talked to us in the locker room," he said. "I'll never forget walking out with him. I lost my dad the year before. And Coach and Coach Roz and everyone were there for me. I put my arm around him. And I told him everything would be okay. I said, 'You were there for me when I lost my dad so if I can do anything for you.' He was crying. We didn't know if he was gonna come back at all that year."

The impact of seeing Olson cry wasn't lost on Murphy. Here was this rock of a man showing his vulnerability. "It's a powerful thing because you see this man that you think can handle anything in life," Murphy said. "He got emotional. I've had a few of those moments with Coach over time. Those are the types of things that last with you forever. You live however many thousands of days in your lifetime. And when one moment like that happens, it impacts like your entire life. You feel it."

A few years later, Murphy had an opportunity to leave to be an assistant coach with Rodney Tension at Loyola Marymount but decided not to go. During that time he had the itch to jump to the NBA and worked camps in Las Vegas. He looked into an internship with the San Antonio Spurs but was content being the UA's director of operations. By then, he was splitting duties with former UA player Reggie Geary. That September he got a call from Warkentien with the Nuggets. He asked if he'd be interested in being the team's video coordinator. "I told Coach O, and he told me it would be a great opportunity," he said. "'If that's what you want to do, you should do it,' and that he'd fully support it. He was awesome."

There are two big things, Murphy said, that made Olson special on the basketball court or at least made a difference in how successful he was: preparation and talent. Olson would handwrite his practice every day, setting aside time in the mornings to get it done. He was not to be interrupted during that time. "He'd have the coaches' meetings in the morning, take notes, and then go back and write practice up," Murphy said. "Once practice was written up, he'd give it to me or Ryan Hansen to type it up. He was detailed. He was meticulous."

Another reason was his ability to know where players would fit where and how to make it work. "He was one of the best ever at it," Murphy said. "He wasn't into talent acquisition like some guys are. He didn't say, 'We have to get this five-star or that five-star.' He understood who could play for him and who the diamonds in the rough were. He knew the players who could make a great team. It wasn't often Arizona was in a recruiting battle with Kansas or Kentucky or this or that. We didn't win many of those even with Coach O. Luke Walton was under the radar. Gilbert Arenas was under the radar. Michael Wright. Coach Olson knew how to put a team together. He'd intermix them with transfers—Ben Davis, Loren Woods—good players. Coach Olson had an eye for talent who could fit his system. He may have been one of the best ever at it."

Neither that ability nor his competitiveness ever waned. Murphy had a seat close by to witness it. "He certainly would get more aggressive during the games with the fans," he said. "I remember the ASU game where he pointed to the scoreboard when the students were giving him grief despite ASU getting crushed...He was as intense in my first year as he was in my eighth year."

That's a reason why Arizona's last-second loss—despite being up big vs. Illinois in the 2005 Elite Eight—was so impactful. "Not many people gave us much stock for a good year, but we won 30 games. It was one of only three teams of his that won 30 games in a season," Murphy said. "You win 30 games and you're having a great year."

But it was a painful loss that everyone will remember. "It was the hardest locker room," he said. "Salim Stoudamire was sitting near his locker and looked physically ill. Channing Frye was physically ill. It was tough. And the toughest locker room I've ever been in...in my lifetime before or since."

Olson was just as impacted as his players as the team flew home from Chicago. "We were last in line at O'Hare Airport waiting to get on the charter home, and his face looked like life had gone out of his body," Murphy said. "From that moment forward, I'm not sure he was ever the same. He never said anything to me, but it was like it was unsaid. He's sitting there thinking that in his mind this may have been his final shot [at a title]. I'm not sure if he really believed that, but at that moment, that's what it felt like."

Three years later Olson retired. A year after the Illinois game, Murphy left for Denver, eventually leaving to become an assistant coach for then-Memphis coach Josh Pastner. In 2012 Murphy became the head coach at Northern Arizona. "I talked to him every few months for sure," Murphy said after he left UA. "I saw him as often as I could, and he came to Flagstaff a lot. His son was a manager for me. There's no better feeling being a head coach, especially at a place like NAU, and have Coach Olson there supporting you. I felt like I was invincible. I didn't feel any pressure. I always had his support."

When he was with Pastner, a former UA player and assistant coach, Olson would show up there, too. "He'd be out there for a few days, watch practice, just spend time with us," he said. "He was always supportive. I know he cared about Damon [Stoudamire] a lot, cared about Jason Gardner a lot, Craig McMillan, Steve Kerr...all his former guys that became head coaches. He loved seeing us coach. He never turned his back on me."

25

Todd Walsh

Few people—former players, friends, managers, or the like—are more grateful to Lute Olson than Todd Walsh. And that's saying a lot. And fewer have had the success he's had in their line of work. Walsh has won 13 Emmys while hosting sports television for a number of networks. His voice and face are familiar for sports viewers in Arizona and beyond. He thanks Olson for giving him a shot at success.

He even considered Olson a father figure. "Heck, I told my dad that," Walsh said. "My dad was born in 1912 so there was a generational gap there, and my dad wasn't around very much. He'd already retired by the time I was in kindergarten. I basically ran away from home and ended up with a guy who was larger than life and someone I didn't want to let down. Lute taught me a lot."

The University of Arizona, the basketball program, and Olson saved Walsh. He first fell in love with Tucson as a 10 year old when his family "slapped a name tag on him" and sent him to visit his older sister back in the mid-1970s. "I'll never forget walking down the steps of the plane and looking up and seeing the desert. It blew my mind and changed my life," he said. "So, I had Arizona tattooed on my mind since that day."

Someday, some way this kid from upstate New York wanted to return to enjoy the weather and the scenery. He also wanted to play baseball. And where better than Arizona? Its baseball team had won the 1980 College World Series. "I never let go of that dream," he said. "When I was a senior in high school, I realized I wanted to be in journalism. So when I picked colleges, it was Arizona or Missouri."

But plans changed. A girl came into the picture. So he sat out a year, and after that didn't work out, he packed up his car that had no air conditioning and drove west. It was the summer of 1983. He often thinks about what would have happened had he not had that gap year. And the girlfriend. And the circumstances. "I still had this dream about playing baseball and I was going to walk on," he said. "I remember walking over there because they were having fall ball and working out. I saw the guys, and they were men. They were men. That's how I saw them. They had just won the title a few years before, and that group would eventually win it again in 1986. So I chickened out."

He also had a problem. He was in deep financial trouble. He'd just arrived at UA with little money and just enrolled in school. He needed to figure something out. "I didn't realize that my room and board weren't included in my tuition," he said. "I had no clue. I had something like $400 to my name."

He ended up washing dishes, serving pizza, and selling his plasma twice a week to survive. "I was in dire straits," he said.

He had an idea: the basketball team may need help with something, anything. And, hey, he had done some public-address work in high school. So maybe the program needed one. "I naively went to McKale," he said, "and knocked on the basketball office."

He spoke to the team's secretary, Jo Pierce, and asked if they needed a PA announcer. "She took pity on me and kind of chuckled and said no," he said, "but that they were putting together a new staff because the school had hired a new coach."

She told him to speak to assistant Scott Thompson. He did and was told to come back in a week for an interview to be a manager. "I didn't know what that meant, but I did it," he said. "As God is my witness, I still have that date on my calendar because it coincided with the 100-year flood in Tucson."

For five days water was everywhere. He had walked a long distance to get interviewed and came in soaked. Because of the flooding, the U of A office provided pizza to those lingering outside and in need. "That was the joke. I was going to get in that line because they served pizza. I was starving," he said. "There were hundreds of kids. So I waited and waited."

There was Thompson again, and he interviewed. Once it was done, he returned to his normal life. "I just went back to school, went back to washing dishes, and serving meals and selling plasma," he said.

He then got a call from Thompson: "He said, 'Congratulations, we need you to come down to the registrar's office so we can reimburse your tuition. You need to turn back your books and get new ones and you need to change your class schedule' and that I was on full scholarship. I don't know how that happened. I don't even know what that meant. But as I've told Coach Olson and Coach Thompson, that changed my life and saved my life."

He still gets emotional talking about it. It was that life-changing and impactful. "There's nothing like walking into a room and lying down on a gurney and having a needle in your arm, later walking out with $25," he said. "I made that $25 last at Der Wienerschnitzel. It's why I get provincial sometimes. I think about that a lot."

That's the reason why he often wrote Olson notes from Phoenix—or from somewhere else in the USA—while covering big sporting events. He appreciated the love while at Arizona. "I'd write what I was doing and how I was doing," he said, "letting him know how he helped me forge a foundation. I wasn't on the floor learning the ways of playing defense or offense, but I learned about preparation; I learned about execution of your job...I was part of the show. This was a high-end program, and you're a part of it in another way. No matter what you do or where you fell in the totem pole, that you had a job, and you were going to be prepared and you're going to execute it."

Walsh carries that mentality to this day. "I've done pregame shows all my career, all major sports, and that's all I've done," he said. "I started to look at shows and my job the way he looked at games. Practice would set you up for that Thursday game or Saturday game. You were always thinking ahead. That turned into my philosophy. There wasn't going to be any surprises. I'm not going to let my island/village down. That started around him. You weren't going to screw up. It didn't matter if it was at practice or whatever. You knew what you had to do. You knew where everybody else had to be."

It helped him have epiphanies. He said he wanted to cover a game at Texas Stadium—and did. He wanted to cover the NBA Finals—and did when the Chicago Bulls played the Phoenix

Suns. He wanted to work a hockey game in Montreal—and did. "I wrote letters to him from wherever I was at," he said.

Walsh was one of many to correspond with Olson in this way. He later found that out after talking to one of Olson's daughters. "I wasn't alone in doing that. He gets these things all the time," Walsh said. "And there's multiple times from the same person same kind of stuff. It makes his day."

Todd Walsh (Courtesy Andy Morales)

In his day job, Walsh often reflects upon the impact his time at Arizona had on him. "Every time I'm out and doing a story and stepping out on the field, I look around and take it in and think how fortunate I am," Walsh said. "It all started at McKale Center and it started with Lute. Even though I never scored a point, had a rebound, or committed a foul in the program, that's how I felt."

When Walsh prepared a speech to perform in front of UA alumni at an event one time, Lute and Bobbi were present. Soon after the speech, Olson went up to him and embraced him. "I just told him I loved him," he said. "It was a huge moment for me. As we were walking out, he said, 'You know we've had a lot of people do a lot of big things and have had some managers take some pretty big steps along the way.' And that I was one…to hear that was great. I was walking on air for a while."

Walsh was a first-hand witness to Cool Hand Lute—as he was dubbed by the media and fans. "I think about the big games we played," he said. "I think about how he acted or presented himself when things were up a notch. I was amazed because the bigger the game, the cooler he got. He calmed everybody down. The guy, who was driving the bus, couldn't wait to get out on the court. He wanted to show what his guys were going to do against your guys. I'd remember him walking on the court, and he had this way about him. People would be bombarding him with insults and verbal tirades [on the road], and he'd just absorb it. I kind of think I can do that in my world. I'm 57 years old now, but at the time, I was 20 years old and watching and absorbing him and what he did. I felt I had the best seat in the house."

Walsh said he "foolishly quit my job" during a tough time in his life. His sister passed, and he was lost. "I remember walking into his office and asking him if he could help me get a job loading cargo planes," he said. "I finally got my head together to get back into the media business in Phoenix when the then-Phoenix Cardinals moved from St. Louis. He was sending letters to my soon-to-be boss. When I got the job, the program director said to me: 'Tell some guy named Lute to stop calling me.' I never knew he did that."

That's what leaders do, and Olson wanted Walsh to succeed. "I've learned in covering sports that leadership matters," he said. "You recognized when you have it and you definitely know when you don't. And I can easily say he was one of the best."

Acknowledgments

Where to begin when you have so many to thank on a project that means so much to so many? You say thanks to all those who contributed and spent time with you—in person, on the phone, or on Zoom—to make this book a reality.

I was able to cover Lute Olson for 17 seasons for the *Tucson Citizen* and spent another 13 as a friend when he retired. As I quoted James Taylor before: "I've seen fire and I've seen rain, I've seen sunny days that I thought would never end."

That was my time with Olson as a reporter given the success he had with Arizona. Olson spent 25 seasons at Arizona—24 years on the sidelines before he took a leave of absence—helping raise the program to new and unfathomable heights in those years. So, there are 25 chapters plus Luke Walton's foreword on his thoughts on Olson and how he helped his career.

Olson brought in some of the best players and people the program had seen in the last half century. So, I figured I'd find some of them, a coach or three, as well as his all-time best player at Iowa (Ronnie Lester). After all, Olson did have a life before Arizona...imagine that.

From great Arizona figures—Steve Kerr to Sean Elliott—to one who started it all, Pete Williams. To Mike Bibby, the freshman guard who helped Olson get his one and only NCAA title, to Damon Stoudamire, an NBA Rookie of the Year. Olson was part father figure/part mentor/part example setter/part coach... and so much more to many of the figures in this book.

Thanks to all of them for their thoughts and personal photos that made this book a reality.

They include the aforementioned as well as: Harvey Mason, Channing Frye, Matt Muehlebach, Matt Brase, Josh Pastner, Reggie Geary, Craig McMillan, Jawaan McClellan, Ben Davis, Jason Gardner, Matt Othick, Jack Murphy, Tom Tolbert, Jud Buechler, Todd Walsh, Jim Rosborough, Mike Montgomery, Roy Williams, and Paul Weitman.

And, of course, thanks to Kelly Olson, who allowed me to write about her husband of more than a decade. She wasn't there for the hundreds of victories but saw the love and admiration those in the book had for her late, great husband.

Finally, to Brenda Baca, a great friend, who was with me through this project and helped me get through an emergency surgery while writing all this. And to my mom, Josie, who continues to be a huge fan.

Thanks to everyone.